Cambridge Primary

Hodder Cambridge Primary

English

Learner's Book
Stage 2

Sarah Snashall
Series Editor: Moira Brown

HODDER
EDUCATION
AN HACHETTE UK COMPANY

The Publishers would like to thank the following for permission to reproduce copyright material:

Acknowledgements

p4, from *When Chico Went Fishing* by Robert Tzannes illustrated by Korky Paul (OUP, 2011), text copyright Robert Tzannes 1994, reprinted by permission of Oxford University Press; p 18, *Clarice Bean, Utterly Me* by Lauren Child (published by Hachette Children's Books); p 40, *Halfway Down* from *Now We Are Six* by AA Milne, text copyright The Trustees of the Pooh Properties 1927, published by Egmont UK Ltd and used with permission; p44 *I'm going on a train* by Sally Grindley from *With Love: A Celebration of Words* compiled by Wendy Cooling (published by Orchard Books); p46, *Choosing Shoes* written by Ffrida Wolfe from *Read Me First: Poems for Young Readers for Every Day of the Year* (published by Macmillan); p86, from *The Monster Sale, Poems by Brian Moses* by Brian Moses published by Frances Lincoln Ltd, copyright 2013, reproduced by permission; p98, p99, p105, p108 from *The Enormous Crocodile* by Roald Dahl (published by Johnathan Cape Ltd and Penguin Books Ltd) reproduced by permission. p 132, *Oomba Bolomba* by Gerard Benson (published by The Poetry Business Ltd) reproduced by permission; p135, from *Even My Eyes are Smiling* by Michael Rosen (published by Bloomsbury Publishing Plc) reprinted by permission; p137, from *Autumn: An Alphabet Acrostic* by Steven Schnur (published by Clarion Books); p137, from *Summer: An Alphabet Acrostic* by Steven Schnur (published by Clarion Books); p140, by Robert Scotellero from *Wild! Rhymes That Roar*, chosen by James Carter and Graham Denton (published by Macmillan).

Every effort has been made to trace all copyright holders, but if any have been inadvertently overlooked the Publishers will be pleased to make the necessary arrangements at the first opportunity.

Although every effort has been made to ensure that website addresses are correct at time of going to press, Hodder Education cannot be held responsible for the content of any website mentioned in this book. It is sometimes possible to find a relocated web page by typing in the address of the home page for a website in the URL window of your browser.

Hachette UK's policy is to use papers that are natural, renewable and recyclable products and made from wood grown in sustainable forests. The logging and manufacturing processes are expected to conform to the environmental regulations of the country of origin.

Orders: please contact Bookpoint Ltd, 130 Milton Park, Abingdon, Oxon OX14 4SB. Telephone: +44 (0)1235 827720. Fax: +44 (0)1235 400454. Lines are open 9.00a.m.–5.00p.m., Monday to Saturday, with a 24-hour message answering service. Visit our website at www.hoddereducation.co.uk

© Sarah Snashall 2014
First published in 2014 by
Hodder Education,
An Hachette UK Company
Carmelite House, 50 Victoria Embankment,
London EC4Y 0DZ

Impression number   10 9 8 7 6 5 4 3 2
Year   2016 2015

All rights reserved. Apart from any use permitted under UK copyright law, no part of this publication may be reproduced or transmitted in any form or by any means, electronic or mechanical, including photocopying and recording, or held within any information storage and retrieval system, without permission in writing from the publisher or under licence from the Copyright Licensing Agency Limited. Further details of such licences (for reprographic reproduction) may be obtained from the Copyright Licensing Agency Limited, Saffron House, 6–10 Kirby Street, London EC1N 8TS.

Cover illustration by Sandy Lightley
Illustrations by Marleen Visser
Typeset in Swissforall in 17pt by Resolution
Printed in India

A catalogue record for this title is available from the British Library

ISBN 978 1471 830 211

Contents

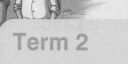

Unit 1 Stories about my world

When Chico Went Fishing

Glossary

fidget
to move hands and feet when sitting still
fishing tackle
the equipment needed to go fishing

One day Chico's father was going fishing.
"Oh, Daddy, may I come too?" asked Chico.
"Please, Daddy? *Please*?"

His father shook his head. "No, son. You're too young. You'll talk too much and scare away the fish. You'll **fidget** and fuss and get in the way." But, seeing the tears in Chico's eyes, he patted his head gently. "Maybe when you're older..."

Then he picked up his **fishing tackle** and set off.

Chico went for a walk. He felt sad. "I *am* old enough to go fishing!" he thought. "I would sit quietly. I wouldn't scare the fish! and I wouldn't get in the way!"

He kept on walking, and soon he reached the river. That gave him an idea.
"I *will* go fishing!" he said. "All by myself. Then they'll see!"

By Robin Tzannes, illustrated by Korky Paul

I can read words using what I know about phonemes and spelling patterns.

I can read and spell words with the **long ee** phoneme.

1 a Are these words new to you? Use what you know about phonemes and spelling patterns to read them.

f-a-th-er   f-i-sh-ing   p-i-ck-ed

2 Practise reading these high frequency words.

one	was	young	come	son	walk	would	enough

a Say the words. Which four words start with a **w** sound? Clue: The spelling of these words don't all begin with **w**!

b Which four words have a **u** sound in them? Clue: They don't all have a letter **u** in the spelling of the word!

3 **ee** and **ea** are two ways that the **ee** phoneme can be spelt. In the story, search for words with the **long ee** phoneme.

a Practise spelling these high frequency words. Write them in two lists. One with **ea** spellings and one with **ee** spellings.

see	tea	been	keep	each	sleep	feet
	queen	please	tree	sea	green	

I can write a sentence with two ideas joined together.

Connecting ideas

1 Write a word with a long ee phoneme for each of these pictures. Remember the ee phoneme can be spelt ee or ea.

⭐ **Helpful hints** ⭐

A good way to join up two parts of a sentence is to use **and**, **but** or **because**.

- **and**
  We can use **and** to add something else to a sentence.

  I like milk **and** I like cheese.

- **but**
  We can use **but** to add something that is opposite to the first part in some way.

  I like milk **but** I don't like cheese.

- **because**
  We can use **because** to explain more about the first part of the sentence.

  I like milk **because** it is cold and creamy.

2 Use **and**, **but**, or **because** to join these sentences together.

a   You'll fidget and fuss _____ you'll get in the way.

b   He picked up his fishing tackle _____ forgot his rod.

c   He kept on walking _____ he wanted to reach the river.

Speech marks

Helpful hints

Speech marks
Speech marks show when someone is speaking in a story. These marks go around the word that the person says.

"Hello" said Dad.

Talk Partners

Practise reading speech marks.
With a partner read the conversation between Chico and Daddy on page 4. Only read the words that are spoken in the story. One of you should be Chico, the other Daddy. If you like, you could change your voice so that you sound like Chico and Daddy!

1 Read these sentences aloud. Try to make it clear when someone is speaking by changing your voice.

a "I want to go fishing!" said Chico.
b The teacher said, "Sit down, please."
c "Thank you!" said the boy.

2 Write out these sentences. Start each sentence with a capital letter. Read the sentences aloud and decide if they are questions or not. At the end of each sentence put either a full stop or a question mark.

a what happened here
b my name is Sacha
c what is your name

I can talk about what happens at the beginning of a story.

Story beginnings

1 Read the extract on page 4.
Can you answer these questions?
Share your answers with a partner.

a Where is Chico's Daddy going?

b How will Chico scare the fish?
Choose an answer.
- He will pull silly faces.
- He will talk too much.
- He will jump up and down.

c How do we know Chico is sad?
Choose an answer:
- He bursts into tears.
- He goes to a friend's house.
- He goes for a walk.

d Find three different words in the story that end with ing.

Helpful hints

The extract on page 4 is the beginning of the story 'When Chico went fishing'. In the beginning of the story:
- You met the main people in the story (Daddy and Chico).
- You found out where they are (Near a river).
- Something happened (Chico decides to go fishing on his own).

Talk Partners

Talk with a partner about what you think will happen next in the story.

a How will he go fishing?

b Will he catch a fish?

c Will he be in danger?

d What will Chico's Daddy say?

What happened next?

1 Here are some ideas about what might happen in the middle and end of the story:

a   Read them all and choose your favourite middle and ending.

b   Write your favourite as one sentence, using and.

Middle	Ending
Chico falls in the water	he finds some treasure
Chico gets scared by a crocodile	he runs home
Chico finds a fishing rod	he catches a fish
Chico meets a friend	he rescues his Daddy
Chico makes a fishing rod	together they go fishing

and

Did you know?

In the real story, Chico makes himself a fishing rod and catches an enormous fish. His Daddy has some little accidents and doesn't catch anything. See if you can find the book and read it in full.
It is written by Robin Tzannes and illustrated by Korky Paul.

Jonah feels tingly

Jonah woke up with a start. Something was happening today. But what was it? He felt tingly. Tingly feelings normally meant good things.

"It can't be a holiday," he thought as he walked down stairs. "Because Dad's gone to work."

"I can't be my birthday," he thought as he ate his breakfast. "Because no one has given me a present."

"School can't be closed," he thought as he tied his shoe laces. "Because I'm in my school uniform and no one thinks that's odd."

Maybe it was the day they give out the parts for the school play. Maybe it was the day they were going on a school trip.

As Mum drove Jonah to school he wondered what could be making him feel like this – all tingly.

"Don't forget, I need you to be first out of the class today," said Mum.

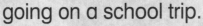

Jonah's heart raced – maybe Mum was taking them to the aqua park. "We have the dentist and it will be a rush to get there on time."

"The dentist! Really? That's what made me tingle? How very disappointing," he thought.

"Don't look so glum, Jonah!" called Mum. "Granny's taking you out for ice-cream afterwards." Granny! Yes, that was it. Granny and ice-cream and probably some extra sweets sneaked when Mum wasn't looking. What a **very** tingly thought.

by Sarah Snashall

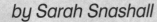

Reading a story carefully

I can answer questions that start with what, where, when, who and why.

I can say who the characters are in a story and where the story is set.

1 Read the story and write the answer to these questions. The start of the first answer has been given to help you.

a Why did Jonah think that something was going to happen today?
(Jonah thought that something was going to happen today because...)

b How did Jonah know it wasn't his birthday?

c How did Jonah know it wasn't a holiday?

2 Read the story on page 10 again.
Write the answers to these questions.

a Who are the two **characters** in the story?

b Which other people are talked about in the story?

c What is the **setting**?

d Where is Jonah going after school?

Glossary

character
a person in a story

setting
the place where the story happens

I can guess at how the characters in the story are feeling.

I can role play part of a story.

My best day

1 With a partner, act out a conversation between Mum and Jonah on page 10. Think about:

a How Jonah feels when Mum talks about the dentist?

b How Jonah feels when he talks about going for an ice-cream with Granny?

2 In groups of four, tell each other about the best day you've ever had (you can make it up if you like). Listen carefully when someone is talking about their good day and ask:

- 'What was your favourite part of the day?'
- 'How did you feel at the end of the day?'

Listen carefully when your group member is talking and don't say anything about your day until it's your turn. When it's your turn, speak clearly and tell your group about your favourite part of the day and how you felt at the end of it.

Talk Partners

With a partner, try to help each other turn your best day into a story with three sentences. Think of your sentences as:

1. Beginning – how the best day started.
2. Middle – what happened.
3. End – how you felt at the end.

3 Now write down the three sentences which describe your best day. Remember to:

- Use what you know about phonemes and spelling patterns. Check to see if the word is on your high frequency word list.
- Use capital letters to start each sentence.
- Use a full stop at the end of each sentence.
- Use **and** to connect two things that happen.

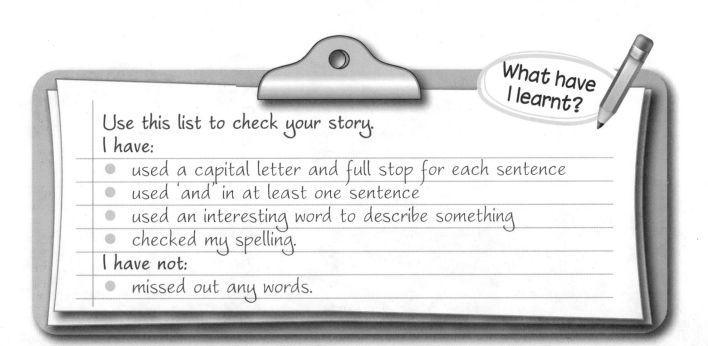

What have I learnt?

Use this list to check your story.
I have:
- used a capital letter and full stop for each sentence
- used 'and' in at least one sentence
- used an interesting word to describe something
- checked my spelling.

I have not:
- missed out any words.

A visit to Auntie's

"Everybody in?" said Dad, cheerily. "Then off we go.
We're going to be nice and early."
Down the road they drove, Mum, Dad, Mei and Chen.
Down the road, round the corner and past the park.
"Auntie is going to love our little cherub!" said Dad.
"The baby! We've forgotten the baby! Turn around!" cried Mum.
Back Dad drove. Past the park, round the corner and down the
road back to the house.
The baby was still asleep in her car seat just by the front door.
Everyone squashed up and she was strapped in the car.
"Off we go, again!" said Dad briskly.
Down the road they drove. Past the park, round
the corner and over the bridge.
"I can't wait to play my violin to Auntie!" said
Chen. "Oh no! Dad, I've forgotten my violin.
We have to go back!"
Back Dad drove. Over the bridge, past the park,
round the corner and down the road back to the house.
Chen ran in, grabbed his violin and got back into the car.

"Off we go, AGAIN!" said Dad crossly.
Down the road they drove. Past the park, round the
corner, over the bridge and along the river.
"I hope Auntie likes the flowers I've made her."
said Mei.
"Oh no! Dad, I've forgotten the present.
We have to go back!"
Back Dad drove. Along the river, over the bridge, past the park,
round the corner and down the road back to the house.
Mei ran into the house and came back with her origami flowers.
"Off we go ... again!" said Dad sadly.
Down the road they drove. Past the park, round the corner, over the
bridge, along the river and finally they
arrived at Auntie's house.
"Here you are at last," said Auntie.
"Did you remember the cake?"

by Sarah Snashall

I can spell words ending in –ly.

Glossary

root word
the original word before it has the suffix added to it. For example, sad + ly

Words ending in –ly

Helpful hints

- An **adverb** is a word that tells us **how** something is done:

  > The man runs quickly along the road.
  > The horse galloped fast.
  > The ball bounces suddenly up in the air.

- A **suffix** is a small group of letters added to the end of a word.

  > slow + ly = slowly
  > quick + ly = quickly

- **-ly spelling rules**
  If the **root word** ends in a y change the y into an i before adding **-ly**

  > happy + ly = happily
  > merry + ly = merrily

1

a   Find these adverbs in the story on pages 14 and 15:

   cheerily   briskly   crossly   sadly

b   Write the root word for each of the above adverbs.

2

Add –ly to these words to make adverbs.
Remember: if the root words ends in y, turn the y into i and then add -ly.

   bad   sweet   happy   soft   brave

Past tense

1 Which of these sentences are in the past tense? Clue: Think whether the sentence is happening in the past.

a   Dad is cross.
b   Dad was cross.
c   Chen plays the violin.
d   Chen played the violin.
e   The baby cries.
f   The baby cried.

2 Write these sentences in the past. You will need to change the verb.

a   I play football.
b   I eat my breakfast.
c   Mum cooks the dinner.

Try this

Write a sentence in the past tense for each of these pictures.

Helpful hints

A verb is an **action** or **being** word. Every sentence needs a verb. For example:

> He **runs** to school.
> ↗verb
> She **is** tall.

The way the verb is written tells us whether the event in the sentence happens now (present tense), will happen in the future, or has happened already (past tense).

> I **skip** along the road.
> ↗ present tense
> I **am** hot today.

> I **skipped** along the road.
> ↖ past tense
> I **was** hot today.

Happy families

This is me, Clarice Bean.
I am not an only child, but
sometimes I wish I was.
My family is six people, which
is sometimes too many.
Not always, just sometimes.
My dad is mostly at the
office answering the phone and
going, "I can't talk now, I'm up to my ears in it."
Mum is always complaining about pants on the
floor and shoes on the sofa.
She says, "This house doesn't clean itself you know.
Who do you think does everything around here?
Mr Nobody?
I don't get paid to pick up your smelly socks!
If I did I'd be a rich woman."

From Utterly Me, Clarice Bean by Lauren Child

Clarice Bean
Clarice Bean lives with her
Mum, Dad, Grandpa, older brother Kurt,
older sister Marcie and younger brother
Minal Cricket. The stories are about her
problems at home and at school.

I can read aloud clearly, taking notice of the punctuation.

Helpful hints

Use punctuation to help your reading sound more interesting.

Question mark

Raise your voice slightly at the end of a question sentence.

Speech marks

These show that the person is speaking in the text. You could use a different voice.

Exclamation mark

This is used to show how the person is feeling. Make your voice match the mood of the person. For example, OH NO! (said loudly!)

Talk Partners

Read the words in the speech bubbles below with a partner. Use the punctuation to make the voices sound different.

I can't talk right now!

Dad

Leave me alone!

Kurt

Where is my phone?

Marcie

Mum. Where are you?

Minal

I don't get paid to pick up your smelly socks!

Mum

My family

 Read these character descriptions of Clarice's family.

Mum

Is tired of listening to her children fight

Clarice Bean

Fights with her younger brother
Gets in trouble when it's not her fault

Minal Cricket

Annoying
Fights with Clarice Bean

Kurt

Likes to be alone
Doesn't talk much

Marcie

Bad tempered
Always on the phone

Dad

Always on the phone

I can write clear sentences using capital letters, full stops and question marks.

I can choose interesting words when I write.

2

a   Draw a picture of someone you are close to – friend or family.

b   Add two labels to the picture that tells us something about them. For example, tall, plays the flute, football fan, funny.

c   Tell a partner about the person you have drawn.

d   After talking to your partner, add extra words to your picture.

3

a   Choose two words you used to talk about your picture from activity 2.

b   Write two sentences about your person using two pieces of information. For example:

- Kurt is silent.
- Kurt is tall.

c   Turn your two sentences into one sentence by using and, but or because. For example:

- Kurt is tall and silent.
- Kurt is funny because he makes jokes.

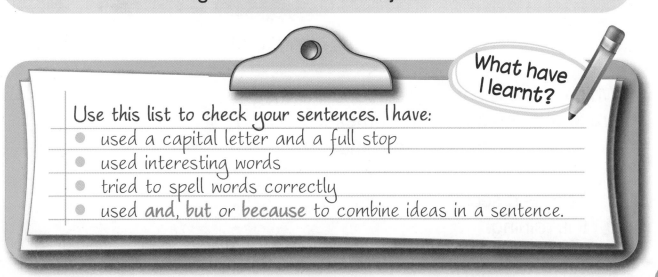

What have I learnt?

Use this list to check your sentences. I have:
- used a capital letter and a full stop
- used interesting words
- tried to spell words correctly
- used and, but or because to combine ideas in a sentence.

Unit 2 Instructions

I know the features of instruction texts.

I know that different texts tell us different things.

Spotting instructions

Helpful hints

Instructions tell us how to do something.
Look for:
- 'What you need' lists
- Numbered points
- Illustrations
- Command words
- Time words

1 Read the titles of these books.
Which books sound like instructions?

How to boil an egg

The Hare and the Tortoise

How to make a space rocket

All about Volcanoes

How to grow plants

2 Which of these sentences sound like they are telling you how to do something?

a Jump up and down ten times.
b I love to drink hot chocolate.
c Tell me a secret.
d It is raining.

How to *draw a silly bird*

I can read and follow a `how to` text.

You will need:
- a piece of paper
- a pen
- paints or crayons
- craft googly eyes
- small pompoms

What to do:

1

Place your hand on the paper with your fingers stretched out.

2

Trace around your hand.

3

Give your bird a beak and legs. Colour in your bird with a colourful pattern.

4

Decorate your bird with googly eyes and pompoms.

Source: Adapted from © Klutz 2005, from *Hand Art* (Klutz)

Reading instructions

I can answer questions about a text.

1 When we write instructions, we use some of the features below to make them easy to follow. Find these features in 'How to draw a silly bird' on page 23.

- A title
- A 'What you need' list
- A list of numbered points
- **Command** (bossy) words. For example:

  | trace | stick | paint |

- Words that tell us **when** to do something. For example:

  | first | then |

- Words that tell us **how** to do something. For example:

  | carefully | quickly |

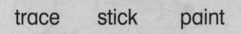

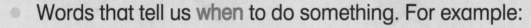

2 Read the instructions and draw your silly bird. Answer these questions.

- **a** What was the first thing you had to do?
- **b** What did you need the pompoms for?
- **c** How did you draw the bird's body?
- **d** How did you give the bird eyes?

The ai and ee phoneme

I know the main spellings for long vowel phonemes.

3 Find words with these spellings in 'How to draw a silly bird'.
a   a_e
b   ai
c   ay

Helpful hints

The **ai** phoneme can be spelt:
- **a_e** as in pl**a**ce
- **ai** as in r**ai**n
- **ay** as in pl**ay**

The **ee** phoneme can be spelt:
- **ee** as in br**ee**ze
- **ea** as in **ea**ch
- **y** as in rain**y**

4 Find words with these spellings in 'How to draw a silly bird'.
a   ee
b   ea
c   y

5 Copy the words below which have the **ai** phoneme in them. Look at the helpful hints box if you need a clue!

stay   play   away
cream   rain   stream   green

25

Command verbs

I can use command verbs.

Helpful hints

Instruction texts use command verbs. Command verbs tell you to do something. For example:

Wash your hands.
Come here.
First, slice the tomato.

1 These sentences tell us to do something. Write down the command verb from each sentence.

a   Follow me.
b   Walk in a line.
c   Add the sugar.
d   Go out to play.
e   Sit down.

2 Write down four command verbs from 'How to draw a silly bird' on page 23.

3 Read these sentences.
Which sentences have command verbs?

a   First break the eggs.
b   Stick the stars on with glue.
c   The girl walks around the corner.
d   Turn right.
e   Carefully fold the piece of paper in half.

Make it clear

1 Choose one of the words or groups of words to make an instruction sentence.

    a   (Listen/He listens/We listen) to the music.

    b   (Write/They write/Ingrid wrote) a story.

    c   (Open/ Alice opened/The wind opened) the door.

    d   (Close/Closing/You will close) your eyes.

2 Write out these sentences adding a command verb for each one.

    a   _____ a book.

    b   First, _____ the eggs.

    c   _____ the football.

    d   _____ the window.

Try this

Turn the sentences below into command sentences. Leave out the person who is doing the action. For example:

> The boy can jump up and down.
> ~~The boy can~~ jump up and down. → Jump up and down.

You might need to change the verb. Say the sentence aloud to yourself to see if it sounds right. For example:

> She bakes a cake. → ~~She~~ bakes a cake. → Bake a cake.

    a   The boys kick the ball.

    b   The mother goes to the shops.

    c   We look after the baby.

    d   The clowns ride the bike.

Writing instructions

I can write instructions.

I can use another text as a model when I'm writing.

1 Look at the pictures below and draw a dragon as shown. Write instructions for drawing the dragon under each picture.
- Give your instructions a title.
- Add a list to show what is needed.
- Use capital letters and full stops.
- Use command words.
- Number your instructions.

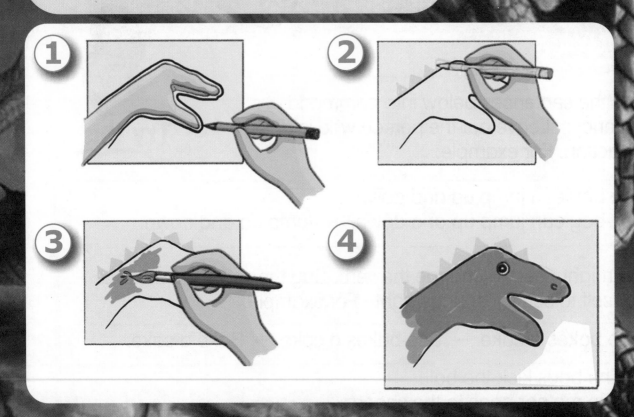

Choose one of these pictures and write a set of instructions to show how to draw it.

Try this

What have I learnt?

Use this list to check your instructions. I have:
- included a 'What you need' list
- used numbered points
- used illustrations
- used command words.

A countryside walk

1 Start at the car park.

Go through the gate, then follow the path until you reach the lake.

2

3 At the lake, turn right.

Look out for Mallard ducks in the lake.

You are back at the car park. **7**

After five minutes you will come to another gate. Go through this. Be careful – it might be slippery.

6

Countryside code
Stick to the paths.
Don't drop litter.
Don't pick flowers.
Don't feed the animals.

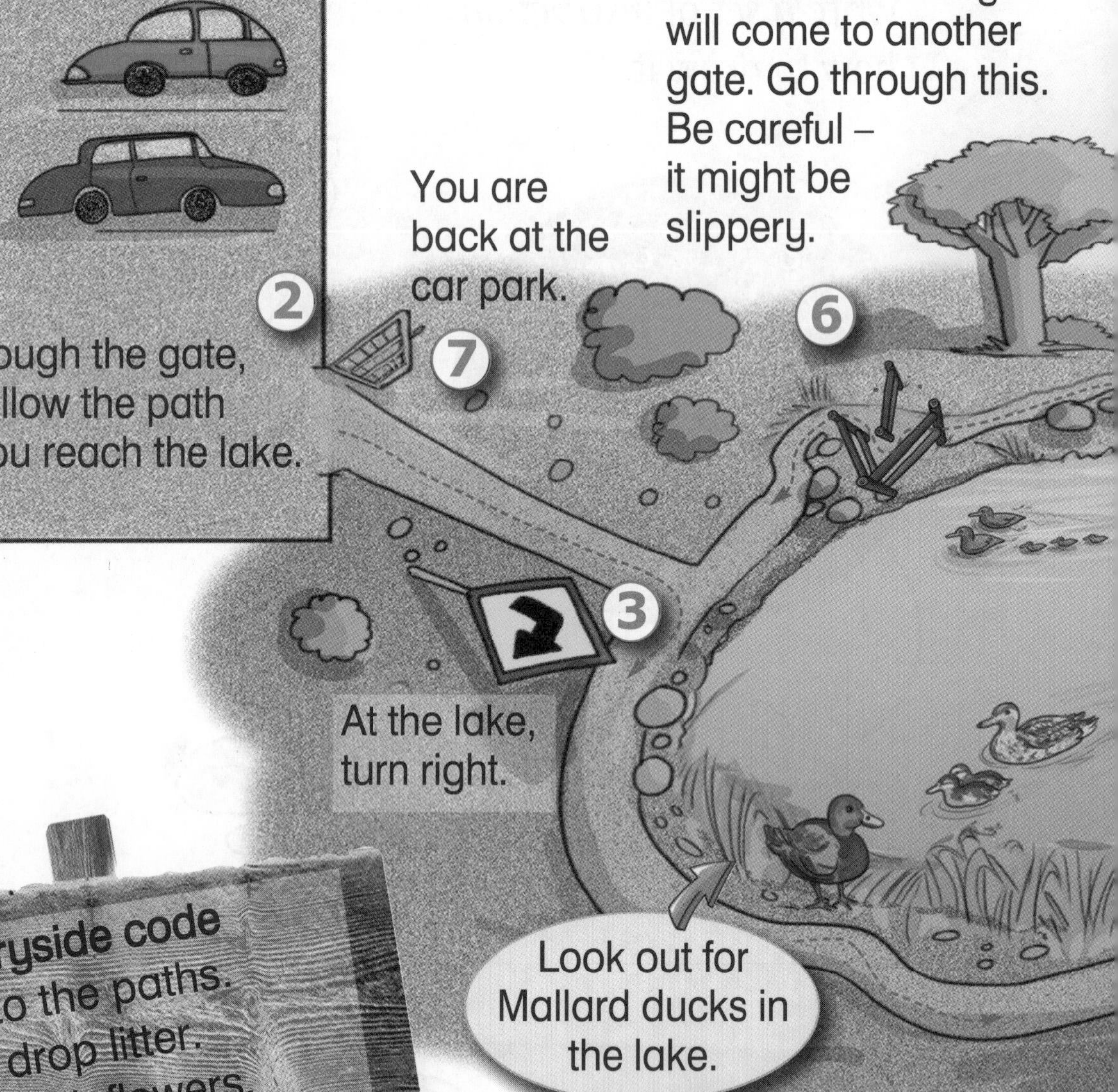

At the end of the path, go through the gate into the woods.

Next follow the path through the woods. Look out for woodland flowers and animals.

A countryside walk

I can find answers to questions by reading the text.

Helpful hints

There are two sets of instructions in 'A countryside walk':
- one tells us how to complete the walk (instructions)
- the other tells us how to behave on the walk (the countryside code).

1 Read 'A countryside walk' and write the answer to these questions.
  a   What can you see on the lake?
  b   How do you get into the woods?
  c   Where does the walk start and end?
  d   What three things should you not do on the walk?

2 Copy these sentences, using the words that show time to complete them.

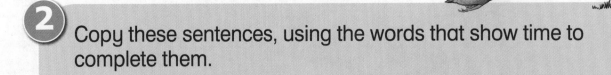

next   then   when   after   sometimes   never

  a   _____ feed the animals.
  b   _____ lunch, go to see Mrs Parker.
  c   Sieve the flour and _____ add the eggs.
  d   Watch out near the lake: _____ the ground is muddy.

3 Words which show time help us to know when to do something. Find two words which show time in 'A countryside walk'.

I can spell words with that end –ly.

Adding –ly

Helpful hints

Remember, words that end –ly often tell us **how** something is done.

Cut up the pizza **neatly**.

The boys ate the ice-creams **greedily**.

The children played **quietly**.

1 Add –ly to these words.
a careful
b quick
c slow
d loud
e nice

2 Write out these sentences adding one of the new words from activity 1.

a _____ cut along the dotted lines.

b Walk along the road _____.

c Add the milk _____.

d The girls sang _____.

e Stroke the cat _____.

33

Giving directions

I can use role play to practise what we're learning.

I can give my classmates clear instructions, speaking so they can understand me.

1 Draw a map of a new walk. Describe your walk to a friend. Use **left** and **right** in your directions if you can.

left   right

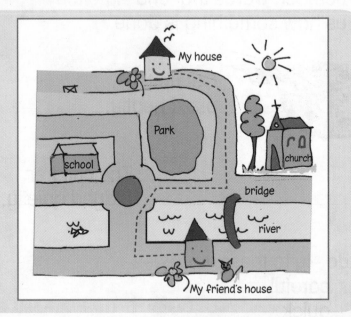

Talk Partners

How to get to my classroom.
A new learner is joining your school. Ask a classmate to pretend to be the new learner. Make him or her feel welcome by giving instructions for how to get to your classroom from the front door of the school.
For example:

Welcome to our school Ben. Let me tell you how to get to our classroom. Please listen carefully. First, go down the corridor, past the office. Turn right. Go up the stairs. Turn left. Your classroom will be in front of you.

More words which show time

1 Write instructions for a new learner to get to their classroom.
Use these words and this order to start your sentences:

1. Hello...
2. First...
3. Then...
4. Then...
5. Finally...

Helpful hints

Try to use one of these words in your instructions.

- carefully
- immediately

Use this list to check your instructions. I have:

- used command words
- added –ly words
- used time words
- used a capital letter and a full stop for each sentence
- checked my spelling.

What have I learnt?

How to play musical statues

What you need:

- Eight or more players
- Music
- A Music Master – an extra person who is in charge of the music and judges the game.

What to do:

1. Get into a large space where everyone can hear the music.
2. The Music Master turns on the music. He or she lets the music play for about a minute and then turns it off.
3. When the music is playing, everyone dances.
4. When the music stops, everyone freezes.
5. Anyone who is still moving after the music stops is out. That person sits down and the music is turned back on.
6. The winner is the last person left.

The players must move their whole body when they dance!

Who, what and where

1 a Which word below does NOT sound like it starts with a **w** sound?

where   when   who   winner   why

b Find the words above in 'How to play musical statues' on page 36. Sound each word out.
c Find a word above that rhymes with **dinner**.
d Find a word above that rhymes with **air**.
e Find a word above that rhymes with **pie**.

2 Answer these questions about 'How to play musical statues'.
a Who is the winner of the game?
b What do you need to play musical statues?
c What should a player do when the music starts?
Use the answers to play musical statues with your friends.

Musical statues

Talk Partners

Teach a group of younger children how to play musical statues. Remember to talk in a way that they can understand. Give them simple instructions. For example:

1 Dance when the music starts.
2 Freeze when the music stops.

1 Make up your own game based on 'musical statues'. For example, when the music stops you have to:

- sit down
- put on a silly hat
- touch the wall.

Writing presentation

Write down how to play the game from activity 1. Remember:

- give your game a title
- tell your reader what equipment they need
- tell them what to do.

Put the games your classmates have written together to make a book.

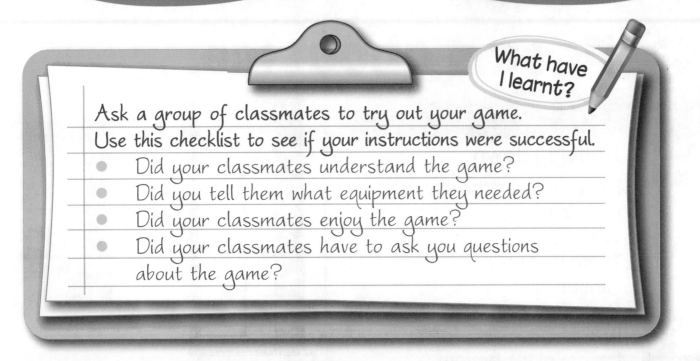

What have I learnt?

Ask a group of classmates to try out your game.
Use this checklist to see if your instructions were successful.
- Did your classmates understand the game?
- Did you tell them what equipment they needed?
- Did your classmates enjoy the game?
- Did your classmates have to ask you questions about the game?

2 Which of these things do you find in a set of instructions?

- a princess
- a heading
- words that rhyme
- command verbs

- numbered sentences
- illustrations
- what you need list
- time words

3 Put these instructions for making pancakes in the correct order.

a   Turn over after one minute. Cook for another minute.
b   Mix together the ingredients in a bowl.
c   Eat your pancakes with lemon and sugar.
d   Heat some butter in a frying pan.
e   How to make pancakes
f   Put half a cup of mixture in the pan.
g   You will need: two eggs, 100 g flour and 250 ml milk.

Unit 3 — Poems about me

Halfway down

Halfway down the stairs
Is a stair
Where I sit.
There isn't any
Other stair
Quite like
It.
I'm not at the bottom,
I'm not at the top;
So this is the stair
Where
I always
Stop.

Halfway up the stairs
Isn't up,
And isn't down.
It isn't in the nursery,
It isn't in the town.
And all sorts of funny thoughts
Run round my head:
"It isn't really
Anywhere!
It's somewhere else
Instead!"

By A A Milne

My special place

1 Answer these questions about 'Halfway down'.
  a Where does the poet like to sit?
  b Find and write the word in the poem that rhymes
  with each of these words:

> stair   sit   top   down

2
  a Read the poem out loud.
  Try clapping along with
  the rhythm.
  b Choose one answer to
  show why you think the
  poet likes to sit halfway
  down the stairs.

> to be quiet

> to dream

> to be alone

Talk Partners Tell your partner about a special place where you like
to be alone. Is there a quiet corner in your home
where you like to hide? Do you sit on your bed?
Now listen as your partner speaks about their
special place. Ask your partner questions and
listen carefully to their answers.

The long oa phoneme

I know different spellings for the oa phoneme.

Helpful hints

1

a Which words in the cloud below have a **long** oa phoneme?

If the word has the letters **ow** in it, be careful. Say the word out loud and listen to the sound of the phoneme. Is it oa as in *snow* or ow as in *cow*?

b Write the words below which have the **long** oa phoneme in a list in your book and underline the letters that make the oa phoneme.

snow   down
town   pot   stop
alone   flown   coat
oak   note

Say the word grow. Can you hear the **long** oa sound? The oa sound can be spelt in different ways. Here are the different spellings for the phonemes:

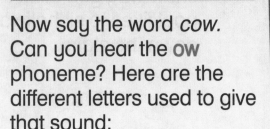

- oa as in boat
- o_e as in stone
- ow as in snow

Now say the word *cow*. Can you hear the ow phoneme? Here are the different letters used to give that sound:

- ou as in cloud
- ow as in clown

2

Find a word in the cloud above that rhymes with these words:

down   alone   coat

The long igh phoneme

1 Copy the words on the stairs. Find a rhyming word in the box to match each word on the stair. Write the rhyming word next to it. Say each word out loud.

cry

below

stone

mine

night

pie

slime

nice

fine
crime
blown
mow
try
slice
my
bite

Helpful hints

Say the word **night**. Can you hear the long **igh** phoneme in the middle of the word? The **igh** phoneme can be spelt in lots of different ways.

- **i_e** as in slid**e**
- **igh** as in l**igh**t
- **y** as in cr**y**
- **ie** as in p**ie**

2 Can you write a word with a **long igh** phoneme for each of these pictures?

Try this

Can you think of another rhyming word for each example in activity 3?

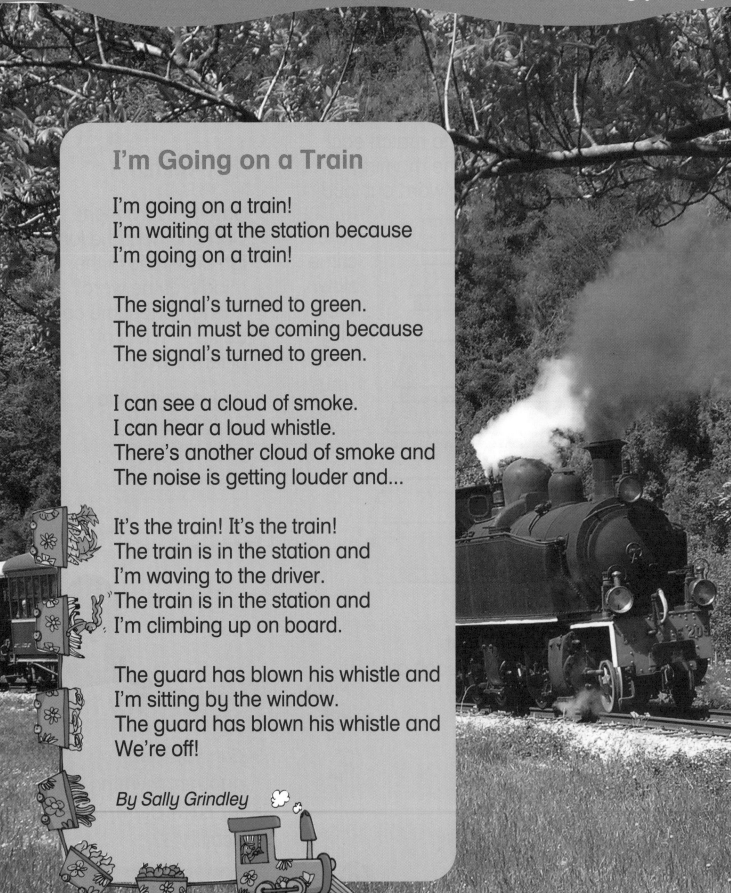

I'm Going on a Train

I'm going on a train!
I'm waiting at the station because
I'm going on a train!

The signal's turned to green.
The train must be coming because
The signal's turned to green.

I can see a cloud of smoke.
I can hear a loud whistle.
There's another cloud of smoke and
The noise is getting louder and...

It's the train! It's the train!
The train is in the station and
I'm waving to the driver.
The train is in the station and
I'm climbing up on board.

The guard has blown his whistle and
I'm sitting by the window.
The guard has blown his whistle and
We're off!

By Sally Grindley

I can use my voice in different ways to make what I'm saying interesting to listen to.

Giving a performance

1 Find all the repeated lines in 'I'm Going on a Train'. Why do you think these lines have been repeated?

2 Draw a punctuation mark to match each description below. Use one of these:

! – an exclamation mark   **.** – a full stop   **...** – an ellipsis.

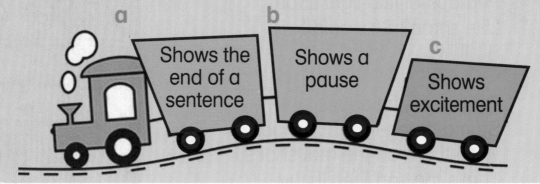

a **Shows the end of a sentence**

b **Shows a pause**

c **Shows excitement**

Talk Partners
Take turns to read the poem aloud to a partner. Try different ways to make the poem interesting.

- Start quiet and get louder as the train gets closer.
- Think about the sound a train makes as it's going along. Try and say the poem in this rhythm.
- Only pause at the end of a line if there is a full stop or an exclamation mark.
- Say the sentences that end in an exclamation mark as if you are very excited.

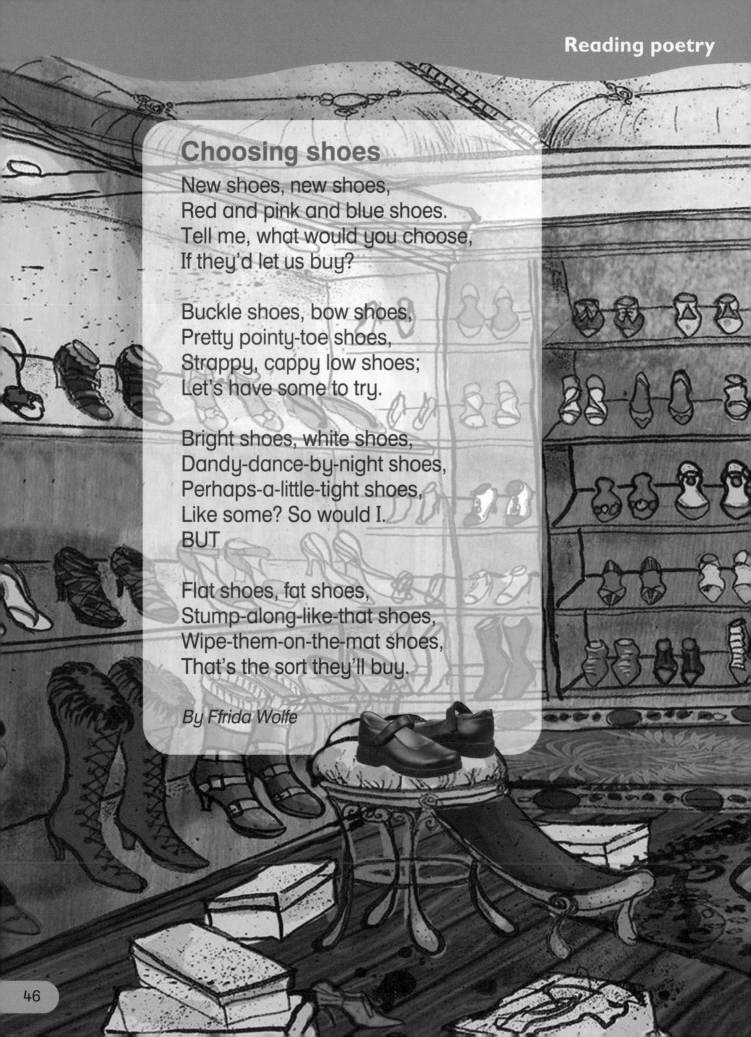

Choosing shoes

New shoes, new shoes,
Red and pink and blue shoes.
Tell me, what would you choose,
If they'd let us buy?

Buckle shoes, bow shoes,
Pretty pointy-toe shoes,
Strappy, cappy low shoes;
Let's have some to try.

Bright shoes, white shoes,
Dandy-dance-by-night shoes,
Perhaps-a-little-tight shoes,
Like some? So would I.
BUT

Flat shoes, fat shoes,
Stump-along-like-that shoes,
Wipe-them-on-the-mat shoes,
That's the sort they'll buy.

By Ffrida Wolfe

Syllables

1 Read 'Choosing shoes' and write the answer to these questions.

a Find the rhyming words in each verse.

b Which of these words describes the shoes that the poet would like to have:

fun   comfortable   wide   **brown**

c Which of these words describes the shoes that the poet thinks she will be bought?

fun   pretty   sensible   pointy

Helpful hints

A syllable is a beat in a word. Clap out the beats in these words:

- cat   cow   horse (These words have one syllable.)
- rabbit   donkey (These words have two syllables.)
- elephant   kangaroo (These words have three syllables.)

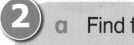

Talk Partners

Tell your partner what you think 'Dandy-dance-by-night shoes' might look like.

Can you describe the shoes and then draw a picture of them? (Dandy is an old word meaning fashionable.)

2 a Find four words in 'Choosing shoes' with:
- one syllable
- two syllables.

b How many syllables are there in:
- 'Dandy-dance-by-night'
- 'Perhaps-a-little-tight'.

Adjectives

Talk Partners

Read the poem on page 46 with your partner. Talk about the words that describe each pair of shoes.

Helpful hints

Words that describe something, someone or somewhere are called adjectives.

- The green frog.
- The bouncy ball.
- The day is sunny.

1 Match adjectives from the list to each of the shoes below:

> spotty   clean   silly   green   tall   sparkly   sporty
> clumpy   stripy   fancy   white   bouncy   dancing   muddy

a

b

c

d
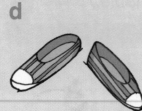

e

f

My shoes

I can write neatly.

I can write a poem based on a poem I've read.

2

a Choose your favourite pairs of shoes from activity 1.

b Write a poem about each pair of shoes by putting an adjective from page 48 on each blank line.

- _____ shoes
- _____ shoes
- _____ _____ _____ shoes

For example:

sporty shoes

strappy shoes

bouncy silly muddy shoes

Writing presentation

Write your new poem for display. Remember:

- Keep your tall letters the same height and your short letters the same height. This will make it easy to read.
- Leave a finger space between the words.
- The letter y should have its main part on the line and its tail below the line.
- Draw pictures around your poem.

My Poem

What have I learnt?

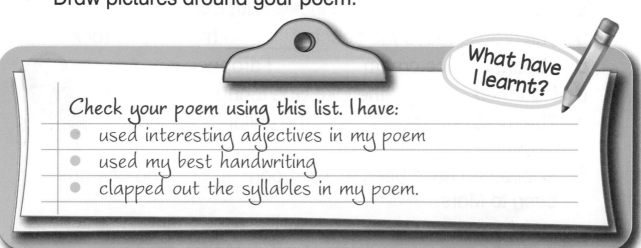

Check your poem using this list. I have:
- used interesting adjectives in my poem
- used my best handwriting
- clapped out the syllables in my poem.

1 Which of these words have one **long igh** phoneme?
Write down the words and underline the letters
that make the **igh** phoneme:

like	fly	I
tried	happy	pin
sight	meat	still

2 Write down how many syllables there
are in these words.

a snapping
b sunflower
c tree
d trainer
e holiday
f seaside
g thunderstorm

3 Which words fit the sentence?
Choose **and**, **but** or **because** to join
the two parts of these sentences.

and   but   because

a I took my coat _____ it looked like rain.

b The crab crossed the beach _____ hid under a rock.

c I bought an ice-cream _____ I dropped it.

d I laughed _____ the joke was funny.

e The music started _____ the children started
to dance.

f Spacemen have been to the moon _____ no one has
been to Mars.

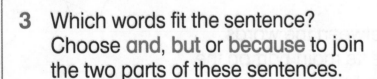

4 Find four pairs of rhyming words in the cloud.

> freeze   crate   heap   sheep   train   skate
> cheese   poke   eagle   beagle   plane   cloak

5 Write down all the adjectives you can find in this text.

> Quiet Tilly sat at the table watching her family. Her family was fun but noisy. There was her older brother John, he was tall and sporty. He was telling a funny story about his football match. Her younger sisters, Emma and Jess were making silly faces at each other. Her grandpa had fallen asleep and was snoring loudly.

6 Complete these instructions for making a sandwich.

Add these missing words:

Next, place, Cut, First, add, bread, tomato, Put, cheese, butter

How to make a sandwich

You will need: _____, _____, _____, _____.

- _____, butter two slices of bread.
- Then, _____ a slice of cheese on the bread.
- _____, _____ a slice of tomato on top of the cheese.
- _____ the other piece of bread on top.
- _____ the sandwich in half.

Unit 4 Tales from around the world

The fool and the donkey

An Iranian folk tale
Once upon a time a **fool** went to buy a donkey. There were many donkeys at the stall. Some were big and some were small. Some had long ears and some very short. But among them there was one donkey that had long, floppy, **silky** ears.

"This is the donkey for me," said the fool.

The fool paid the stall holder. He put a rope around the donkey's neck and led the donkey away through the streets of the town.

Two naughty boys watched him. Their names were Amir and Nouri. Amir was the older boy, and liked to be in charge.

"Let's play a trick on that fool, and steal his donkey," said Amir to Nouri. And he told Nouri his plan.

Glossary

fool
a silly person

silky
very soft and smooth

Nouri went up to the donkey and carefully took the rope from around the donkey's neck and put it around his own. He then followed the fool in the donkey's place.

Meanwhile, Amir sold the donkey back to the donkey seller. He skipped for joy when he saw the money he was given.

Nouri followed the fool out of town. When the fool reached his home he turned to the donkey. "Aahh," he cried. "When I bought you, you were a donkey. But now you've turned into a boy!"

"It's true, I was a donkey but I'm really a little boy. I was rude to my mother and she turned me into a donkey. Now I have turned back into a boy. But you have bought me and I belong to you."

"You belong to me?" said the fool. "I cannot own a boy. Go, but promise never to be rude to your mother again."

The next day, the fool realised he still needed a donkey. Taking his last few coins he went back to the donkey stall. Among the donkeys he noticed there was one donkey with long, floppy, silky ears. He knew that donkey. He went over to it and he lifted its ear and said: "You foolish boy, I said never be rude to your mother again!"

Retold by David Heathfield and Sarah Snashall

The long oo phoneme

1

a Read the words below.
All these words have the **long oo** phoneme in them.

rude   fool   true   new
tune   pool   blue   crew
cute   hoot   clue   newt

Sort the words out into a table with four columns like this:

u_e	oo	ue	ew
cute	hoot	clue	newt

b Can you think of another word to go in each column of the table?

Helpful hints

Say the word *fool*. Can you hear the **long oo** phoneme in the middle of the word? The **oo** phoneme can be spelt:

- **oo** as in f**oo**l
- **u_e** as in r**u**d**e**
- **ue** as in bl**ue**
- **ew** as in st**ew**.

Try this

Choose two words from the table and use them to write a sentence. For example:
- The new baby is cute.
- I hung my blue hat on the hook.

54

2 **a** What phonemes and spelling patterns do these words use?

> short   name   floppy
> long   donkey   silky

b Find the words above in the story on pages 52 and 53 and read the whole sentence.

Helpful hints

Remember:
* First look for the phonemes in the word.

  f-oo-l
* Next, blend the phonemes together to read your word.

f-oo-l...
fool

3 Re-read 'The fool and the donkey' on pages 52 and 53 and write down the answers to these questions.

a What three words are used to describe the donkey's ears?

b What happens to the donkey?
* The fool takes it home.
* The donkey is stolen.
* It runs away.

c What does Amir do with the donkey?
* He sells it.
* He gives it to his mother.

d Read the last two lines of the story again. Who does the fool think the donkey is?

Beginning, middle and end

1 Read these events from the story.

- The fool sends him away.
- Two boys steal the donkey.
- The fool goes to buy another donkey.
- A fool buys a donkey.
- A boy pretends to be the donkey.

Do these events happen at the beginning the middle or the end of the story? Write the events in the correct order under these headings:

Beginning one event	**Middle** three events	**End** one event

Talk Partners

Use the Beginning, Middle and End boxes from activity 1 to re-tell the story to your partner.

Use the boxes to remind you of what happens in the story.

Give the two boys the names of you and your partner.

Use these phrases to start your story.

Beginning: Once upon a time...

Middle: Two naughty boys ...

End: So, then the fool ...

I can say what the setting is in a story.

I can say what the characters are like.

Who's in the story?

1 Choose two words from the box below to describe Nouri and two words to describe the fool.

> clever   trusting   kind
> foolish   naughty

a    b

2 Which of these two settings are in the story?
- A big modern city
- A town a long time ago
- A house near a town
- A duck pond

3 Find two clues in the story that tell us it is set a long time ago.

Helpful hints

- A **character** is a person in a story.
  There can be lots of characters in a story.

- A **setting** is where and when a story happens. There can be more than one setting in a book.

A box of sweets

There once was an Emperor of India called Akbar who had three foolish advisors and one clever one. One day he decided to test them. He walked into his throne room looking very cross. "I have just had my hair pulled!" he cried. "I have caught the person who did it! What shall we do with him?"

"This is a disgrace!" said the first **advisor**. "Throw him in the deepest dungeon."

"This is terrible!" said the second advisor. "Send him into the widest desert."

"This is the worst thing I've ever heard!" said the third advisor. "Make him sleep with the smelliest of animals."

"Very interesting ideas," said the Emperor. He turned to his wise advisor:

"Birbal, what do you say?"

The wise advisor smiled and said, "I think he should be given a box of sweets."

"Are you mad?" said the first advisor.

"Are you ill?" said the second advisor.

"Are you crazy?" said the third advisor.

"Not at all," said Birbal. "There's only one person who would pull the Emperor's hair: his grandson… ."

By Sarah Snashall

There are lots of stories about Akbar and his clever advisor, Birbal. They were real people and lived in India about 450 years ago.

Glossary

advisor
someone who helps the Emperor make decisions

Reading difficult words

I can use phonics to read words I don't know.

I can see where the speech marks are and show that someone is talking.

I can read a story clearly.

Talk Partners

Read the words in the box with a partner. First find the phonemes and spelling patterns in the word. Then blend the sounds or patterns together.
For example:
looking (l-oo-k-ing)   throw (th-r-ow)

| disgrace | crazy | Emperor | India |

1 Find all the speech marks in the story. Work with a partner.
One of you should read all the spoken words.
The other should read the rest of the story.

2 a Find these high frequency words in the story. These words just need to be learnt because their spelling is unusual.

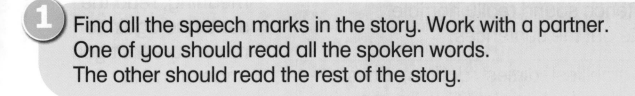

| once | one | eyes | walked | all | would |

b In the box above:
  • Which letter has been added to *one* to make it *once*?
  • Which word sounds the same as 'wood'?
  • Which word starts with the long igh phoneme?

I can talk about the meaning of new words.

I can use adjectives to describe a setting.

Story language

1 Match up the words to their meaning.

Word	Meaning:
disgrace	• a place with little or no rain
dungeon	• a large, special chair for a ruler of countries
desert	• a shameful thing
throne	• an underground prison

2 Choose an adjective (describing word) from the box to make the setting in the sentence sound really horrible. Write out the sentences.

> smelliest, dirtiest, darkest, driest, dampest, snake-filled, freezing, man-eating, scariest

a   Throw him in the _____ dungeon.
b   Send him into the _____ desert.
c   Take him to the _____ forest.
d   Leave him in the _____ swamp.
e   Lock him in the _____ tower.

Helpful hints

If you don't know the meaning of a word:

- see if you can work out the meaning from the sentence
- ask someone if they know what it means
- see if the word is in the glossary.

After learning the meaning, read the sentence again to make sure that you understand it.

The parts of a story

1 Write a sentence to explain what happens in the beginning, middle and end of the story on page 58.

Beginning	Middle	End

2 Choose which of the following statements describe Birbal or the foolish advisors.

a   Men who talk before they think.

b   A man who can think like a detective.

c   Men who get cross quickly.

d   A clever man.

Talk Partners

Pretend you and your partner are the foolish advisors talking together afterwards.

• How do you feel?

• What do you say to each other?

• Are you cross, sorry or jealous of Birbal?

• Do you think that the Emperor tricked you?

How the Zebra got his stripes

Long ago, when the world was new, there was a great big baboon, who sat by the **waterhole** and frightened away anyone who came near the waterhole to drink. He lit a fire to frighten the lions and tigers.

One day a zebra came to the waterhole. He was all white and his fur shone in the sunshine.

The baboon, who was sitting by his fire, jumped up. "Go away," he barked. "This is my waterhole."

"The water is for everyone," shouted back the zebra.

"If you want it, you must fight for it," snarled the baboon. **In a heartbeat** the zebra and the baboon were fighting. Back and forth they went, until with a mighty kick, the zebra sent the baboon flying high up onto cliff behind them. The baboon landed with a smack on his bottom.

The kick was so strong that zebra fell backwards through the baboon's fire. This burned him, leaving black stripes across his white fur. The zebra ran away to the **plains** where he has stayed every since. The baboon still lives on the cliffs. He barks crossly at all strangers and holds up his tail so that the air can cool his sore bottom.

Glossary

waterhole
a pool where animals come to drink

in a heartbeat
at once

plains
a large area of grassland

I can suggest what characters might be thinking.

I can answer questions about a story.

1 Can you answer these questions about the story?

a Where and when is the story set?

b Which two adjectives are used to describe the baboon in the first sentence?

c What colour is the zebra's coat at the beginning of the story?

d What happened to the zebra after he kicked the baboon?

e How did the zebra get his stripes?

2 a What does the baboon think at the beginning of the story? Choose one of these thoughts.

I will share this water with all the animals.

This is my water.

b What does the zebra think when he first meets the baboon?

That's his water.

That's not fair.

I can split compound words into parts.

Compound words

1 The two words that make up a compound word help us to understand what the compound word means.
For example:
A goalkeeper keeps balls out of the goal.

Split each compound word below into the two words that make it.

a   waterhole
b   anyone
c   sunshine
d   heartbeat
e   fireside

Helpful hints

A compound word is a word made up from two words, for example:

- sunflower (sun+flower)
- ladybird (lady+bird)
- greenhouse (green+house)

2 Find five compound words in this passage.
Write each one out as two words.

Alan the anteater woke up. He was hungry and he needed something to eat. He waddled across the grasslands in search of termites. On the way he met Grant the grasshopper and together they set out to look for breakfast.

Adjectives

1 Add one of these adjectives to each sentence to make it sound more interesting.

Helpful hints

An adjective is a word that describes something.
- The pretty hat.
- The silver car.
- The fun day.

> dirty hot white stripy scary
> cross big high tall

a The zebra fell into the _____ fire.
b The zebra had _____ fur.
c The zebra fought the _____ baboon.
d The baboon went to live on the _____ cliff.

2 Write an adjective to describe each of these animals.

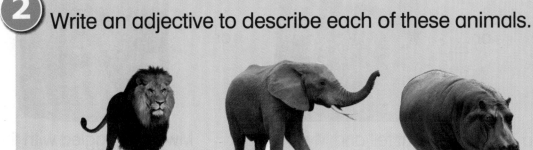

lion   elephant   hippo   giraffe

Try this

Write a sentence about each animal in activity 2. Use adjectives to make the sentences more interesting. Remember to use a capital letter and a full stop.

Mwenda makes the stars

Read these ideas for a story about how the stars were made.

Beginning

In the first days there were no stars. At night it was so dark that you couldn't see your hand in front of your face.

There was a girl who lived at that time called Mwenda. She liked running around in the wilderness on her own.

One day Mwenda found a pile of diamonds.

Middle

or

or

She met a tiger who wanted her diamonds. She threw them into the sky to hide them from the tiger.

Night fell and Mwenda got lost. She threw the diamonds up into the sky to light her way home.

Mwenda juggled with the diamonds. She threw them too high and they didn't come down.

End

That night all the people of the earth saw the stars. These were Mwenda's diamonds in the sky.

Writing a story plan

1 Copy boxes like the ones below to plan your version of 'Mwenda makes the stars'. Use the questions to write notes. Notes don't need to be sentences, just important words.

Beginning
Mwenda finds diamonds.
Where does she find the diamonds?
Write your ideas.

Middle
Mwenda throws the diamonds into the sky.
Why does she do this?
Write your ideas.

End
Mwenda's diamonds become the stars.
How does this happen?
Write your ideas.

Talk Partners Use your notes to tell the story to a partner. Then listen carefully to your partner's version of the story. Make sure you look interested as they are speaking. Ask your partner to tell you what's good and what could be improved about your story. Give them helpful ideas about their story.

Improving the story plan

1 Think about the feedback your partner gave you about your story. Make notes on your story plan to show how you could make it better.

2
a Choose a story opening to add to the plan.
For example:
  • Once upon a time ...
  • At the beginning of time ...
  • There once was ...
b Think of some adjectives for these words in your story:
  • Mwenda
  • the diamonds
  • the night sky
  • the stars.
Add the adjectives to your story plan.

My story plan

Beginning
Once upon a time ...
Mwenda finds diamonds.
by rocks

Middle
Mwenda throws the
glittering diamonds into
the sky.
meets tiger
Mwenda scared
Tiger wants diamonds

End
Mwenda's diamonds become
the **shiny** stars.
everyone has a party

Try this

Think of something that Mwenda might say in the story. Add this to your story plan. For example:

"What's that under the rock?" asked Mwenda.
"These are my diamonds!" shouted Mwenda.
"Oh no!" cried Mwenda.

> I can read my story to make sure that it makes sense.

3 Use your plan to write the story.
Try to spell the words you know correctly.

> light,
> l-igh-t

- First say the word and try and work out the phonemes or spelling patterns.
- Write the separate phonemes or spelling patterns to complete the word.

Writing presentation

Use your best handwriting so others can read your story. Remember to make your letters neat and round. Make sure your letters all sit on the line. Look at these books.

My Story

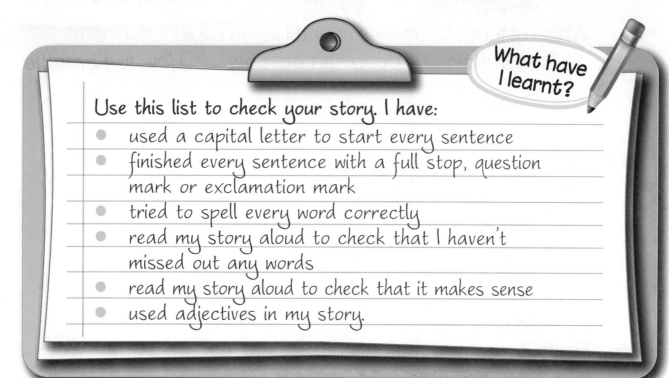

> What have I learnt?

Use this list to check your story. I have:

- used a capital letter to start every sentence
- finished every sentence with a full stop, question mark or exclamation mark
- tried to spell every word correctly
- read my story aloud to check that I haven't missed out any words
- read my story aloud to check that it makes sense
- used adjectives in my story.

Unit 5 Amazing plants

I know that different texts tell us different things.

Explanation texts

1 They are all explanations.

a   Find the word 'How' or 'Why' in each title?

How rainbows are made

Why we don't fall off the earth

How a sunflower grows

Why insects can stand on water

Helpful hints

Explanation texts tell us:
- **How** something happens
  - How frogs grow
  - How I became a footballer
- **Why** something happens
  - Why ice floats
  - Why we should eat healthy food

b   Which of these book titles sound like an explanation text?
- *The Gruffalo*   • *Deep sea animals*   • *How fish breathe*

Talk Partners   With your partner, think of a question each of you need answering.

- First, think of a subject you are interested in. For example, animals or football.
- Next, think of something about the subject you want to know more about. For example, endangered animals or a special footballer.
- Finally, turn your subject into a 'why' or 'how' question: Why are pandas dying out? How did David Beckham become a great footballer?

How a sunflower grows

A sunflower grows from a seed into a flowering plant. The middle of the flower has lots of seeds which then become new plants.

The life-cycle of a sunflower

1 A sunflower seed is pushed into the earth.

2 In the summer a seed germinates. The roots grow down and the shoot grows up.

shoot

root

6 The flower dies and turns into a seed head. The seeds then fall to the ground.

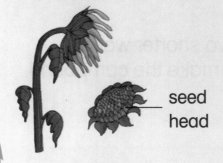

seedling

seed head

bud

3 A small shoot comes out of the soil and grows into a seedling.

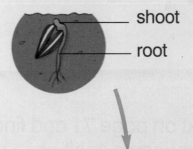

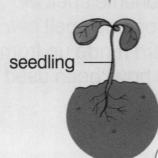

4 A seedling grows into a tall plant. Flower buds grow on the plant.

5 The buds open and the sunflowers are large and yellow.

Glossary

bud
a new flower before it opens

germinate
to start growing when the time is right

life-cycle
the stages that a living thing goes through

seedling
the tiny plant that grows out of the seed

shoot
the first green point that comes out of the ground

Exploring words

Helpful hints

The **long** ee phoneme can be spelt:

- **ee** as in f**ee**t
- **ea** as in **ea**t
- **y** as in happ**y**

The **long** oa phoneme can be spelt:

- **oa** as in c**oa**t
- **o_e** as in h**o**m**e**
- **ow** as in cr**ow**

1   a   Look at the text on page 71 and find two words with:
- a **long** ee phoneme spelt **ee**
- a **long** oa phoneme spelt **ow**.

   b   A compound word made up from two shorter words. What two words have been used to make the compound word *sunflower*?

2   Find these high frequency words in 'How a sunflower grows' on page 71. Use what you know about phonemes and spelling patterns to read the words below. The first has been done for you.
- small (sm-all)
- grow
- down
- up
- off

3 Read these words.

frown	house
crown	mouse
crowd	loud
bow	mountain

Helpful hints

The **ow** phoneme can be spelt:
* **ou** as in gr**ou**nd
* **ow** as in fl**ow**er

Practise trying to spell them.
* Ask a partner to say the word without you looking at it. Say the word and try and work out the separate phonemes.
* Write the separate phonemes. For example, f-r-ow-n.
* Check the word against the spelling. If you got it wrong, practise writing it a few of times.
* Remember: the end of mountain says 'ten' but is written **tain**.

s-ou-n-d
sound

ow can be spelt ow or ou but I think *sound* is spelt with ou.

4 Choose a science word from the cloud to go with each of these pictures. Look at the text on page 71 for help.

seed   germinate   root   seedling   bud   head

a   b   c   d   e   f

73

Labels and captions

Explanations use different features to make the information easy to read.

I can find information from different parts of a text.

a heading (what the page is about)

an introduction

How a sunflower grows

A sunflower grows from a seed into a flowering plant. The middle of the flower has lots of seeds which then become new plants.

The life-cycle of a sunflower

1 A sunflower seed is pushed into the earth.

2 In the summer the seed germinates. The roots grow down and the shoot grows up.

shoot

root

6 The flower dies and turns into a seed head. The seeds then fall to the ground.

3

a diagram (a drawing, picture or graph)

seedling

seed head

A small shoot comes out of the soil and grows into a seedling.

a label (usually on a diagram)

bud

4 A seedling grows into a tall plant. Flower buds grow on the plant.

a caption (some text about the diagram)

5 The buds open and the sunflowers are large and yellow.

Glossary

bud
a new flower before it opens
germinate
to start growing when the time is right
life-cycle
the stages that a living thing goes through
seedling
the tiny plant that grows out of the seed
shoot
the first green point that comes out of the ground

1
a Find a word beginning with **r** that is a label.
b What is the introduction used for?
c What is a diagram? Choose one answer:
   • a seed   • a picture   • a plant
d What is the heading?

I know what to look for in explanations.

2 Find the answers to these questions in 'How a sunflower grows' on page 71. Look at the labels and headings around the picture for clues.

   a What word is used to say that a seed has started to grow?

   b What is the part of the plant that grows downwards?

   c Which part of the plant makes the new seeds?

   d What must happen to the plant before the seeds can fall to the ground?

3 Choose one of these new words to complete these sentences:

> germinate   lifecycle   seedhead

   a When the flower is dead and covered in seeds it is called a _____.

   b In the summer a seed in the ground will begin to _____.

   c The _____ of a frog is frogspawn, tadpole, frog.

Did you know?

The world's tallest sunflower was grown in Germany in 2012. It was 8.23 m tall. Sunflower seeds are eaten as snacks and used to make cooking oil.

I can find out information from websites.

I can make notes by writing down key words.

The lifecycle of a butterfly

1

a With a partner, talk about what you know about how a butterfly grows. Write what you know about butterflies under the heading 'What we know'.

b Now talk about what you need to find out. You may need to know:
- where the butterfly lays its egg
- what comes out of the egg
- what is the special home it makes
- when the butterfly comes out of its special home.

Write notes under the heading 'What we want to find out'.

Helpful hints

When you write notes, only write down the important words called **key words**.

For example, you don't need to write 'Butterflies lay their eggs on a leaf.'
Just write: 'Butterfly – eggs – leaf'.

2 Use the internet or a non-fiction book about butterflies to find the answers to your questions in activity 1. Write notes about what you've found out under the heading 'What we have learnt'.

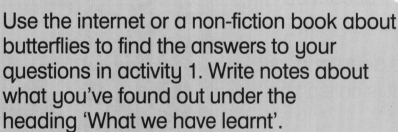

A butterfly presentation

1
- Get **four** pieces of card. Write one of these key words on each card: **egg** **caterpillar** cocoon butterfly
- Draw a stage of the butterfly's life on each card.
- Now write a sentence on the back of each picture explaining what happens at that stage of the butterfly's life.

2
With your partner, use your cards from activity 1 to tell the rest of the class about the lifecycle of a butterfly.
- Decide who is going to say each card.
- Practise holding up the pictures and reading the sentence on the back. Talk loudly and clearly.
- Give your presentation to the class.
Start off by saying: 'Today we would like to tell you about how a butterfly grows'.

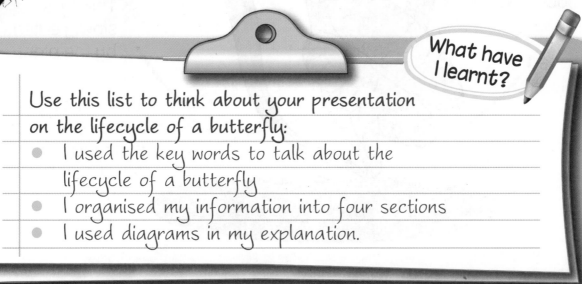

What have I learnt?

Use this list to think about your presentation on the lifecycle of a butterfly:
- I used the key words to talk about the lifecycle of a butterfly
- I organised my information into four sections
- I used diagrams in my explanation.

How a Venus Flytrap catches flies

Killer plants

A Venus Flytrap is a plant that grows where the **soil** is poor. To get the things it needs to grow it catches flies.
How can it do this with no feet or teeth?

Glossary

soil
the earth that a plant can grow in
nectar
sweet liquid made by plants

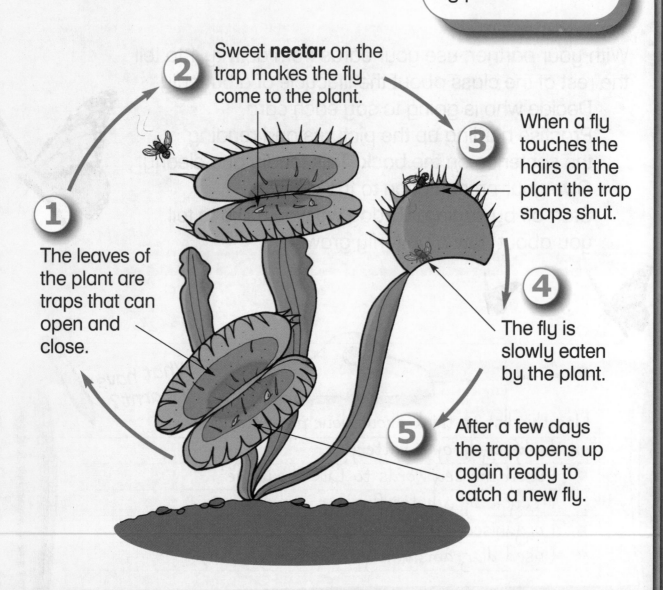

2 Sweet **nectar** on the trap makes the fly come to the plant.

1 The leaves of the plant are traps that can open and close.

3 When a fly touches the hairs on the plant the trap snaps shut.

4 The fly is slowly eaten by the plant.

5 After a few days the trap opens up again ready to catch a new fly.

Finding information

1 Read 'How a Venus Flytrap catches flies' to answer these questions.

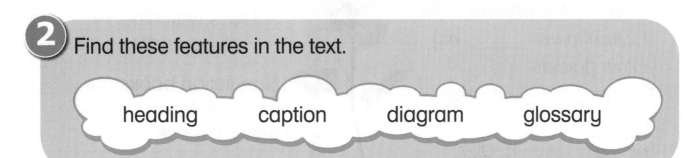

a When does the trap close?
  • When a fly touches a hair on it.
  • Every few days.
  • It opens and closes all the time.

b Why does the fly land on the plant?
  • Because the plant is green.
  • Because the plant has sweet nectar for the fly to eat.
  • Because it is tired.

c Why does the Venus Flytrap eat flies?
  • Because it has teeth.
  • Because it likes them.
  • Because there is no goodness in the soil where it lives.

d What happens when the trap has eaten the fly?
  • The trap opens again.
  • The trap dies.
  • The plant grows a new trap.

2 Find these features in the text.

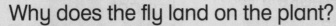

heading   caption   diagram   glossary

The present tense

1 Which two sentences are written in the present tense?
   a   The trap shuts.
   b   Yesterday, the fly flew away.
   c   The trap opens again.

2 Write out these sentences choosing the right verb to make the sentence the present tense.
   a   The lion **has/had** big teeth.
   b   The girl **was/is** late for school.
   c   The flower **grows/grew** very tall.
   d   The chair **was/is** green.
   e   Dad **cooks/cooked** the dinner.

Helpful hints

- When sentences say what is happening now, we say they are written in the present tense.

> The boy **kicks** the ball.
> The fly **lands** on the plant.
> I **am watching** TV.
> She **is riding** a bike.

- When sentences tell us about things that have already happened in the past, we say they are written in the past tense.

> The boy **kicked** the ball.
> The fly **landed** on the plant.
> I **was watching** TV.
> She **was riding** a bike.

Non-fiction books are often written in the present tense.

Try this

Fill in the missing word word to complete these sentences in the present tense.
   a   The sunflower _____ big yellow flowers.
   b   The cat _____ with the widow.
   c   The bee _____ nectar.

New words

1 Match each word in the cloud below to the correct definition (meaning of words).

> Venus Flytrap   soil
>
> nectar   heading

a   sweet sugary liquid made by plants
b   earth that plants grow in
c   words at the top of a piece of writing that tell you what it's about
d   a plant that catches flies

Helpful hints

A **glossary** is a list of the difficult words in a book and what they mean (definition).

A **definition** is a sentence that tells you what a word means.

Talk Partners

Words in a glossary are often in alphabetical order. With your partner, put the words in the cloud in activity 1 into alphabetical order.

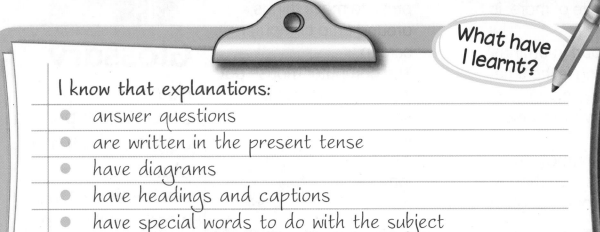

What have I learnt?

I know that explanations:

- answer questions
- are written in the present tense
- have diagrams
- have headings and captions
- have special words to do with the subject
- have a glossary to explain what the special words mean.

Dictionaries

m ▶ moon

M m

moon *noun*

The moon moves round the Earth once every twenty-eight days. You can often see the moon shining in the sky at night.

more

More means a larger amount of something. *There is more water in a lake than a pond.* The opposite of more, is less.

morning *noun* (mornings)

The morning is the time from the beginning of the day until twelve o'clock noon.

mother *noun* (mothers)

A mother is a woman who has a son or a daughter.

motorbike *noun* (motorbikes)

A motorbike is a kind of heavy bicycle with an engine.

motorway *noun* (motorways)

A motorway is a very wide road, made so that traffic can move fast.

mountain *noun* (mountains)

A mountain is a very high hill. *There is snow on top of the mountain.*

mouse *noun* (mice)

1. A mouse is a very small animal with a long tail and a pointed nose.

2. A mouse is also a small box with buttons that you press to move things around on a computer screen. *The computer mouse got its name because it is small and looks like it has a long tail.*

M

the type of word

the word used in a sentence

the definition (the meaning of the word)

the plural of the word

extra information

Glossary

noun
a word for a person, a place or a thing

plural
the version of the word used when there is more than one

Adapted from Oxford First Illustrated Dictionary *compiled by Andrew Delahuntly*

1 Look at the dictionary page opposite.
a   Which word comes after *motorway*?
b   Which word means 'the time from the beginning of the day until 12 o'clock noon'?
c   What is the plural of *mouse*?
d   Find a definition to go with these pictures:

2
a   Find *moon* and *mouse* in your class dictionary.
b   Read the definitions.

Try this

a   Write a definition for the words below.

| bed | car | hat |

Say what you do with the object and why, but do not use the name of the object.
b   Read the definitions to your partner. Can they guess what the word is?

Helpful hints

To find a word in a dictionary:
• First find the section for the first letter of your word.
• Then look for words with the same first and second letter of your word.
• Finally look at the words with the same first, second and third letter.

• Search the words until you find your word.
• Read the definitions and any examples.
• If there are two definitions for your word, read them both and decide which is right for your word.

Joining sentences

1 Look at the diagram of a pitcher plant. Talk to your partner about how it might catch a fly.

The Killer Pitcher Plant

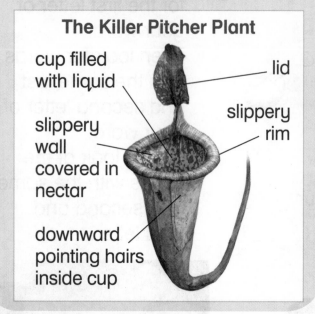

cup filled with liquid

lid

slippery wall covered in nectar

slippery rim

downward pointing hairs inside cup

2 Use **but**, **then**, **because** or **so** to complete these sentences. Use each word once.

a   The fly lands on the plant _____ it smells nectar.

b   The plant smells nice _____ it's a trap.

c   The fly slips on the rim _____ falls into the cup.

d   The sides of the plant have hairs that point down _____ the fly can't crawl out.

⭐ **Helpful hints** ⭐

We can join ideas in sentences in different ways.

• **and** – use **and** to add another point.

> A plant needs light and water to grow.

• **then** – use **then** when one thing happens after another.

> First the root grows then the shoot.

• **but** – use **but** when the second part of the sentence is different from what you might expect.

> She watered the plant but it didn't grow.

• **so** – use **so** to say when the event in the first half of the sentence causes the event in the second half of the sentence.

> There were no buses so she walked home.

• **because** – use **because** when the second half of the sentence explains why the first half happened.

> The plant grew because it had been watered.

I can use headings, captions and diagrams to make the information easy to find.

3 Draw a poster about how a pitcher plant catches flies. Include these features in your poster.

- A main heading: How a pitcher plant catches flies.
- A smaller heading: The plant that drowns flies.
- A diagram: copy the diagram on page 84.
- Captions for your diagram: use the sentences from activity 2 on page 84.
- A glossary: with definitions for 'nectar' and 'rim'.
- Use coloured pencils to make the poster look interesting.

What have I learnt?

Use this list to check your poster. I have:

- used a heading
- used a diagram
- used **but**, **then**, **so** or **because** to link ideas
- used captions
- added a glossary
- used colours to make my poster look attractive.

 Unit 6 Favourite poets

A Good Scary Poem Needs

A haunted house,
a pattering mouse.
A spooky feeling,
a spider-webbed ceiling.
A squeaking door,
a creaking floor.
A swooping bat,
the eyes of a cat.
A dreadful dream,
a distant scream.
A ghost that goes BOO
and You!

By Brian Moses

Did you know?

This poem is a **list poem**. List poems are a good way to give readers lots of description about what something is like.

Fantastic adjectives

1

a Find a word in the poem that rhymes with each
of these words:

> mouse   feeling   door   dream   BOO

b Sort the words in the list above (including the rhyming words
you've found) into the columns below. Write the headings
and put each word in the right column.

ow	ee	or	oo
flower	feet	for	bloom

c Add these words into the correct columns:

> proud   scout   bead   least   your   four   dew   value

Talk Partners

What makes the
poem scary?
The nouns or the adjectives?
Read this poem with a partner
and compare it with the poem
on page 86. The nouns have
stayed the same but the
adjectives have all been
changed. Compare each line in
this poem with those in the
original poem. What is
different?

A sunny house,
   a velvet mouse.
A cosy feeling,
   a white-washed ceiling.
An open door,
   a polished floor.
A cricket bat,
   a tabby cat.
A magical dream,
   an excited scream.
A friend that goes BOO
   and You!

Using new words

I can read and spell words with the **long ur** phoneme.

1 Practise reading and spelling these words with the **ur** phoneme.

> stir   fur   earth   twirl   first
> herb   curl   pearl   kerb

a First look for the phonemes in the word, then blend them together to read the word.

g-ir-l

b Now say the word to yourself and count the phonemes on your fingers. Then write down each phoneme to spell the word.

g-ir-l

Helpful hints

Say the word **f**ur.
Can you hear the **ur** phoneme at the end?
Sound it out:
f-ur.
The **ur** phoneme can be spelt:

- **ir** as in g**ir**l
- **ur** as in h**ur**l
- **ear** as in h**ear**d
- **er** as in t**er**m

Remember: In the words **word** and **work** the **ur** phoneme is spelt **or**.

2 Practise reading the **ur** phoneme in these sentences.

a The first girl to the pearl was the girl with a curl.

b The furry hat looked great with her curly hair.

c Have you heard a word I've said?

d Your work is to stir the soup and add the herbs.

e The seedling pushed up through the earth and uncurled.

f The cat purred and the bird heard.

A wood that is frightening

1 Look at the picture of a wood that is frightening. Choose an adjective from the box to go with each of the nine words.

> pattering, spooky, scary, squeaking, creaking, swooping, dreadful, awful, glowing, creeping, crawling, howling, sneaking.

2

a Write down a list of nine frightening objects and adjectives. For example:
  - a dreadful tower
  - a dark wood
  - a hooting owl
  - a howling wolf.

b Choose your favourite six lines from the list.

c Choose one of these lines to finish your poem:
  - I'm not staying here!
  - This is where I want to be.

d Write out your poem and draw a picture to go with it.

tower

owl

wood

branches

wolf

web

eyes

lizard

spider

Jonathan Jo

Jonathan Jo
Has a mouth like an "O"
And a wheelbarrow full of surprises;
 If you ask for a bat,
 Or for something like that,
He had got it, whatever the size is.

 If you're wanting a ball,
 It's no trouble at all;
Why, **the more that you ask for, the merrier** –
 Like a **hoop and a top**,
 And a watch that won't stop,
And some sweets, and an **Aberdeen terrier**.

 Jonathan Jo
 Has a mouth like an "O,"
But this is what makes him so funny,
 If you give him a smile,
 Only once in a while,
Then he never expects any money!

 By A. A. Milne

Glossary

the more... the merrier
the more we have the happier we are

hoop and top
an old fashioned children's toy

Aberdeen terrier
a type of dog which is small and friendly

Rhyme and rhythm

1

a Read the poem on page 90 with your partner a few times to make sure you can read it smoothly.

b Try clapping the beat as you read the poem together. Try this rhythm: Clap every time part of the word is underlined. Read the poem so the claps are even.

> Jonathan Jo
> Has a <u>mouth</u> like an "<u>O</u>"
> And a <u>wheel</u>barrow <u>full</u> of sur<u>pris</u>es;
> If you <u>ask</u> for a <u>bat</u>,
> Or for <u>some</u>thing like <u>that</u>,
> He had <u>got</u> it, what<u>ev</u>er the <u>size</u> is.

c Clap out the syllables in Jon-a-than Jo.

2

a Find the words in the poem that rhyme with these words.

| surprises | merrier | funny |

b Which words are spelt the same at the end?

Did you know?

A A Milne
This poem *Jonathan Jo* is written by Alan Alexander Milne, the same poet who wrote 'Halfway down' on page 40. He also wrote the stories called *Winnie the Pooh* in 1926. These stories are about his son, Christopher Robin Milne, and his toys.

Voices of Water

The water in the rain says   *Tick Tick Tack*

The water in the sleet says   *Slush*

The water in the ice says   *Crick Crick Crack*

The water in the snow says   *Hush*

The water in the sink says   *Slosh Slosh*

The water in the tap says   *Drip*

The water in the bath says   *Wash Wash*

The water in the cup says   *Sip*

The water in the pool says   *Splish Splash*

The water in the stream says   *Trill*

The water in the sea says   *Crish Crash*

The water in the pond...   *stays still.*

The water in the soil says   *Sow, Sow*

The water in the cloud says   *Give*

The water in the plant says   *Grow, Grow*

The water in the world says   *Live*

By Tony Mitton

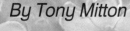

I can use my voice in different ways.

I can speak clearly so everyone can understand me.

Speaking loudly, speaking softly

1 Read 'Voices of Water' with a partner. Answer these questions.
  a   What does the water in the sink say?
  b   What does the water in the sea say?
  c   Which phrase is repeated in each line?
  d   Where is the water that says 'Grow, Grow'?

Helpful hints

In the poem on page 92, some of the words in the poem tell us the sound that the water makes. For example, slosh, splosh, crick, crack, tick. Imagine the water making these different sounds as you read them.

2 Perform 'Voices of Water' with a partner. Practise different ways of saying it. Try these ideas out.
  •   One of you say the words 'The water in the ... says' and the other says the answer.
  •   Say some of the words quietly (hush, drip) and others loudly (crish, crash).
Speak loudly and clearly so that everyone can hear each word.

I can choose interesting words when I write.

The children say...

1 Write a poem about the things that children say. Copy each line and then add an idea from the box below, or use an idea of your own.

The children in the morning say... *Five more minutes!*
The children at breakfast say...
The children in the classroom say...
The children in the playground say...
The children at home time say...
The children in the evening say...
The children at night say...   *Goodnight*

Munch, munch! Carry my bags! Hop, skip and jump!
I don't have a pencil! Miss! Miss! Wheee! Pass it!
Tig! Hooray! Hooray! I don't want to go to bed!

2 Read your poem from activity 1 to a partner. Check it using the list on page 95.

Check the poem you have written.

- Ask your partner to read your poem and give you advice.
  Read your partner's poem and give them feedback.
- I have used the best words.
- I can read my poem aloud.
- I have spelt the words correctly.

3 Choose words from the box or use your own ideas to complete this poem about a rainy day.

> howl crash splash wet pitter-patter drum-drum whoosh
> "Let's stay home"   "Let's go outside"

a The wind says _____
b The rain says _____
c The puddles say _____
d I say _____

4 Draw an illustration to go with the poem. You could then compare your poem and drawing with a partner. How are the poems different?

1 Write down the two words that make up these compound words:

    a sunflower   **b** somebody   **c** upstairs
    d lifecycle   **e** daylight

2 Read this story:

There once was a tortoise and a hare who decided to have a race. They set off together. Hare zoomed off but the tortoise plodded on slowly step by step. Before long the hare was tired and sat down for a rest.
He closed his eyes for just a moment and was soon asleep. While he slept the tortoise plodded on step by step and won the race.

    Say if these sentences are from the beginning, middle or end of the story.
    a The tortoise won the race.
    b The hare and the tortoise decided to have a race.
    c The hare fell asleep.

3 There are nine adjectives in the passage below. Can you find them all? Write them down.

Jacob walked into the woods. It was dark and spooky. A white owl swooped down over his head and he walked into sticky spider's webs. He was tired and hungry and frightened. He was about to cry when he saw the bright lights of a little cottage.

4 Sort these words into two boxes:
    a words with an **oa** phoneme as in *snow*
    b words with an **ow** phoneme as in *how*.
    Say the word out loud first.

now   crow
low   found
sound   flower
no   pillow

5 Three of these sentences are in the
past tense and three are in the present tense.
Which ones are in the past tense?

a The sunflower is very tall.
b Yesterday, the fool bought a donkey.
c The nectar is sweet.
d Zebras have black and white stripes.
e A long time ago, Mwenda threw the diamonds into the sky.
f Last week, we had a party.

6 Put these words into alphabetical order.

nice   seed   foot   bag   grain   across

7 Read the titles of these books.
Write *fiction* or *non-fiction* for each one.

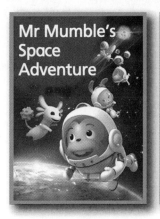   

Mr Mumble's Space Adventure

All about frogs

The Pony Party

How to be the best skateboarder

a   b   c   d

8 Read the words in the box and hear the phonemes and spelling
patterns in them. Put these words into rhyming pairs.

please   sky   rain   high   jam
croak   poke   cram   plane   cheese

The wonderful Roald Dahl

The Enormous Crocodile

In the biggest brownest muddiest river in Africa, two crocodiles lay with their heads just above the water. One of the crocodiles was enormous. The other was not so big.

"Do you know what I would like for my lunch today?" the Enormous Crocodile asked.

"No," the Notsobig One said. "What?"

The Enormous Crocodile grinned, showing hundreds of sharp white teeth. "For my lunch today," he said, "I would like a nice juicy little child."

"I never eat children," the Notsobig One said. "Only fish."

"Ho, ho, ho!" cried the Enormous Crocodile. "I'll bet if you saw a fat juicy little child paddling in the water over there at this very moment, you'd gulp him up in one gollop!"

"No, I wouldn't," the Notsobig One said. "Children are too tough and chewy. They are tough and chewy and nasty and bitter."

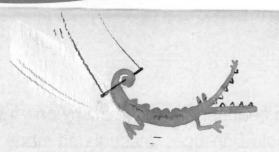

"*Tough* and *chewy!*" cried the Enormous Crocodile. "*Nasty* and *bitter!* What awful tommy-rot you talk! They are juicy and yummy!"

"They taste so bitter," the Nostobig One said, "you have to cover them with sugar before you can eat them."

"Children are bigger than fish," said the Enormous Crocodile. "You get bigger helpings."

"You are greedy," the Notsobig One said. "You're the greediest croc in the whole river."

"I'm the bravest croc in the whole river," said the Enormous Crocodile. "I'm the only one who dares to leave the water and go through the jungle to the town to look for little children to eat."

"You've only done that once," snorted the Notsobig One. "And what happened then? They all saw you coming and ran away."

"Ah, but today when I go, they won't see me at all," said the Enormous Crocodile.

"Of course they'll see you," the Notsobig One said. "you're so enormous and ugly, they'll see you from miles away."

The Enormous Crocodile grinned again, and his terrible sharp teeth sparkled like knives in the sun. "Nobody will see me," he said, "because this time I've thought up secret plans and clever tricks."

From The Enormous Crocodile By Roald Dahl

The best words

Talk Partners

Listen to your teacher read the story on pages 98 and 99. Roald Dahl uses unusual and made up words in his story. Find these words in the story and decide with your partner what they mean.

Notsobig   gollop   tommy-rot   croc

1 Roald Dahl uses lots of adjectives in his story. Adjectives make a story more interesting. Search the story on pages 98 and 99 and find the adjectives that are missing from these sentences.

a   The _____ Crocodile.

b   "I have _____ plans and _____ tricks."

c   The _____ _____ _____ river in Africa.

d   Children are too _____ and _____ .

Helpful hints

Words can be split into syllables. Clap out the syllables in these words.

- clean: <u>clean</u>
  – one syllable
- river: <u>ri-ver</u>
  – two syllables
- muddiest: <u>mudd-i-est</u>
  – three syllables

2 How many syllables are there in these words? Say the words out loud and clap for each syllable.

- crocodile
- enormous
- children
- Notsobig
- chewy

I can say who the characters are in a story and where it's set.

I can guess how the characters in the story are feeling.

Character and setting

1
  a What is the setting for the story?
  b The two crocodiles talk about what children are like to eat.
     Which one of these descriptions is not in the story?

- tough and chewy
- nasty and bitter
- tasty and sweet
- juicy and yummy

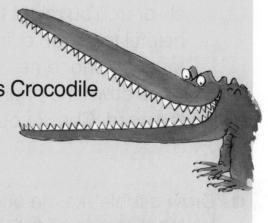

  c Roald Dahl says that the Enormous Crocodile
     has teeth 'like knives in the sun'.
     How does this make him sound?
     Choose one of these words:

     frightening   cross   shiny   tall

  d When is the story happening – in the past or the present?

2 Choose one of the words to answer each question.
  a How do you think that the Enormous Crocodile feels
     when he thinks about catching children?

     excited   scared   puzzled

  b What do you think the Notsobig Crocodile thinks
     about the Enormous Crocodile's plan?
- He thinks he's brave.
- He thinks he's silly.
- He thinks he's mean.

The park in the dark

1 Say the word *charm*. Can you hear the *ar* phoneme in the middle?

a Practise spelling words with the **ar** phoneme.

sharp art bar carpet start

- Say the word.
- Listen for the phonemes in the word, for example: ch-**ar**-m. You might find it helpful to put up a finger for each phoneme.
- Write down the phonemes to spell the word. Check your spelling.

ch-ar-m

Helpful hints

Remember:
- The **ar** phoneme is usually spelt **ar** as in:
  p**ar**k d**ar**k h**ar**p

2 a Draw a table like the one below. Write the words from the box in the table under the right heading.

cream sleep car are slice shy rain plane sharp today crocodile chewy nice lay eat

ee phoneme	ar phoneme	igh phoneme	ai phoneme
cream		shy	

- The **ee** phoneme can be spelt:
  ee as in s**ee**
  ea as in s**ea**t
- The **igh** phoneme can be spelt:
  i_e as in m**i**n**e**
  y as in fl**y**
  igh as in t**igh**t
- The **ai** phoneme can be spelt:
  ai as in tr**ai**n
  ay as in st**ay**
  a_e as in cr**a**n**e**

Reading aloud

> I can read aloud clearly, taking notice of the punctuation.

1 Read the story on pages 98 and 99 aloud in a group of three. Choose a role:

Person 1: reads the words of the *Enormous Crocodile*

Person 2: reads the words of the *Notsobig Crocodile*

Person 3: reads the words of the *narrator*.
(These are the words that are not said by one of the characters.)

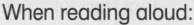

Helpful hints

When reading aloud:
- Read clearly and not too fast.
- Read loudly so that everyone listening can hear you.
- Imagine you are the crocodile or the narrator.
- Every few lines, try to look at the people listening to you.

Talk Partners

Talk about the following questions and share your ideas:

a What 'secret plans and clever tricks' do you think the Enormous Crocodile has?

b What do you dislike about the story?

c This is the opening of the story. Do you want to know what happens next? Why?

The first trick

The Enormous Crocodile crept over to a place where there were a lot of coconut trees.

He knew that children from the town often came here looking for coconuts. The trees were too tall for them to climb, but there were always some coconuts on the ground that had fallen down.

The Enormous Crocodile quickly collected all the coconuts that were lying on the ground. He also gathered together several fallen branches.

"Now for Clever Trick Number One!" he whispered to himself. "It won't be long before I am eating the first part of my lunch!"

He took all the coconut branches and held them between his teeth.

He grasped the coconuts in his front paws. Then he stood straight up in the air, balancing himself on his tail.

He arranged the branches and the coconuts so cleverly that he now looked exactly like a small coconut tree standing among the big coconut trees.

Soon, two children came along. They were brother and sister. The boy was called Toto. His sister was called Mary. They walked around looking for fallen coconuts, but they couldn't find any because the Enormous Crocodile had gathered them all up.

"Oh look!" cried Toto. "That tree over there is much smaller than the others! And it's full of coconuts! I think I could climb that one quite easily if you help me up the first bit."

Toto and Mary ran towards what they thought was the small coconut tree.

The Enormous Crocodile peered through the branches, watching them as they came closer and closer. He licked his lips. He began to dribble with excitement.

From The Enormous Crocodile By Roald Dahl

1 Read the next bit of the story. Answer these questions.

a What is the Enormous Crocodile's Clever Trick Number One?

b Where does his plan take place?

c What are the names of the two children?

d What does the Enormous Crocodile do when the children come towards him?

e Why does the Enormous Crocodile hold leaves in his mouth?

2 Look at this picture of the crocodile. Write two sentences to describe him. Use the words in the labels to help you.

Thinking of secret plans and clever tricks.

Dribble

Teeth like knives

Try this

Write a sentence to describe how the Enormous Crocodile looks when he is pretending to be a coconut tree.

I can spell words that begin with **un-**.

I can spell words that end **–ly.**

Adding -ly and un-

1 Find three words in 'The first trick' on pages 104 and 105 that end in **-ly**.

2 Add **un-** to each of the words below. Then match each word with the picture.

a safe	b done	c happy
d tidy	e lock	

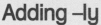

Helpful hints

Adding –ly
- We can add **–ly** to the end of some words to give us words that describe how something is done.

| slow+ly = slowly |
| kind+ly = kindly |

Adding un-
- We can add **un-** to the beginning of some words to make them say the opposite.

| un+happy = unhappy |
| un+kind = unkind |

1

2

3

4

5

1 Get into a group of four and act out the story of 'The first trick' from pages 104 and 105. Choose a role:

- Narrator (story teller)
- the Enormous Crocodile
- Toto
- Mary

Talk about how it will end with your group.
Choose an ending for your role play.

2

a Read how the children are saved from 'Clever Trick Number One' below.

b Do your role play again with this ending.

c Which ending do you like best?

Suddenly there was a tremendous whooshing noise. It was Humpy-Rumpy, the Hippopotamus. He came crashing and snorting out of the jungle. His head was down low and he was galloping at a terrific speed.

"Look out, Toto! shouted Humpy-Rumpy. "Look out, Mary! That's not a coconut tree! It's the Enormous Crocodile and he wants to eat you up!"

Humpy-Rumpy charged straight at the Enormous Crocodile. He caught him with his giant head and sent him tumbling and skidding over the ground.

"Ow-eeee!" cried the Crocodile. "Help! Stop! Where am I?"

Toto and Mary ran back to the town as fast as they could.

From The Enormous Crocodile
By Roald Dahl

3 Read these ideas for a new trick.
  a Choose an idea from the red box and match it to the yellow box.
  b Share the ideas you matched with a partner. Write down your final ideas.

The Enormous Crocodile	But
• sets up a sweet shop • pretends to be a see-saw • pretends to be a bridge • dresses up as the school headmaster	• it begins to rain and the children go home • a clown arrives and the children run off to see it • a park ranger comes and saves the children • but an elephant comes along and crushes it

4 Now make a cartoon strip to show your ideas from activity 3. First plan out the trick by drawing the four stages of it.

Beginning	Middle	Middle	End
Draw your idea from the red box above.	Draw a picture of the children arriving at the trick.	Draw a picture of someone arriving at the trick.	Draw a picture of your idea from the yellow box above.

Making characters talk

1 a Look at your clever trick cartoon strip from page 109. Think of something for the characters to say in each picture. Here are some ideas:

> **Beginning:** The crocodile thinks of his trick. He thinks about how hungry he is and how nice the children will taste.
> **Middle:** What do the children say when they see the see-saw or the thing that the crocodile has created?
> **Middle:** What does the person or animal that arrives say?
> **End:** What does the crocodile say?

b Practise telling the story three times to yourself, trying out some different ideas for what people say. Then write a speech or thought bubble for each of your pictures in the cartoon strip.

Oh look! A new sweet shop.

Ow! Ow! Ow!

Yummy. I'll soon have a tasty snack.

Watch out! That's a crocodile!

2 Roald Dahl uses lots of words for sound effects in the story. Add some of these words to your cartoon strip. Write it above your picture where something noisy happens.

crash   crack
bang   crunch
slurp   thud
hooray   whumph
ooooowwwww

Suddenly!

I can use words which show time.

Helpful hints

Words that show time
Time words tell us when things happen. There are lots of time words to choose from:

- first
- one day
- then
- suddenly
- on Monday
- the next day
- next
- finally
- at last
- soon
- before long.

1 Use the words to fill the gaps below. They must be in the right order for the story.

Before long	At once	First
then	Now	

"_____ for Clever Trick 99," said the Enormous Crocodile. _____ he put on his mother's hat, _____ he put on his mother's classes and then he put on his mother's dress. He sat on a log and got out his mother's knitting. _____ the children came out to play. "Hello children" he said in his best grandma's voice. "Who would like to learn how to knit?" _____ the children gathered round.

2

a Look at your clever trick cartoon strip from page 109. Tell the story to yourself again and look out for places where you could add a word to show time to each part of the story. Add a time word under each box of the cartoon strip.

b Re-tell your story, using the time words and the words that the characters say.

111

Longer sentences

> I can use different words to join ideas and move my story along.

Helpful hints

Time words can move a story along. Linking ideas in a sentence can also move a story along. The most important words to join parts of sentences are and, because, so and but.

1 Use and, because, so or but to fill in the gap in these sentences.

  a   The Enormous Crocodile wanted to eat children _____ they taste good.

  b   The Enormous Crocodile was about to eat Mary _____ Humpy-Rumpy arrived to save her.

  c   The Enormous Crocodile's trick didn't work _____ he had other tricks to try.

  d   Mary and Toto were in the woods _____ they wanted to pick coconuts.

2 Return to your cartoon strip of the Enormous Crocodile's new trick. Write a sentence underneath each picture in the story.
  • Start your sentence with a word that shows time.
  • Use and, then, so or because in one of your sentences.

3 Your clever trick cartoon strip is nearly finished. You should now have a picture with a speech or thought bubble and a sentence for each of the four stages of the story.

- Now write a second sentence underneath each picture to tell more about what happens.

We can write different types of sentences which need different punctuation.

Make one of your new sentences:

- a **statement**, for example:
  There are crocodiles in the lake.
- a **question**, for example:
  Who will save the children?
- a **command**, for example:
  Keep on the path.
- an **exclamation**, for example:
  At last! Silly Mr Crocodile!

What have I learnt?

Use this list to check your cartoon strip. I have:
- written a story with a beginning, a middle and an end
- used words that show time in my story
- used one question in my story
- used one exclamation in my story
- used and, but, so or because in my story
- spelt the words correctly
- used a capital letter at the beginning of a sentence and the right punctuation at the end.

Enormous Crocodile play script

The two crocodiles sit in a muddy river in Africa.
One is very large and mean; the other is smaller.

Enormous Crocodile: Do you know what I would like for my lunch today?

Notsobig One: No. What?

Enormous Crocodile: [*Grinning*] For my lunch today, I would like a nice juicy little child.

Notsobig One: I never eat children, only fish.

Enormous Crocodile: Ho, ho, ho! I'll bet if you saw a fat juicy little child paddling in the water over there at this very moment, you'd gulp him up in one gollop!

Notsobig One: No, I wouldn't. Children are too tough and chewy. They are tough and chewy and nasty and bitter.

Enormous Crocodile: Tough and chewy! Nasty and bitter! What awful tommy-rot you talk! They are juicy and yummy!

Notsobig One: They taste so bitter, you have to cover them with sugar before you can eat them.

Enormous Crocodile: Children are bigger than fish. You get bigger helpings.

Notsobig One: You are greedy. You're the greediest croc in the whole river.

Enormous Crocodile: I'm the bravest croc in the whole river. I'm the only one who dares to leave the water and go through the jungle to the town and look for little children to eat.

Notsobig One: You've only done that once. And what happened then? They all saw you coming and ran away.

Enormous Crocodile: Ah, but today when I go, they won't see me at all.

Notsobig One: Of course they'll see you. You're so enormous and ugly, they'll see you from miles away.

Enormous Crocodile: Nobody will see me, because this time I've thought up secret plans and clever tricks.

Adapted from The Enormous Crocodile, by Roald Dahl

Reading a play

Helpful hints

Look for these things when reading a play:
- the character talking
- the words they say
- what can be seen on stage

> Enormous Crocodile: Do you know what I would like for my lunch today?
>
> Notsobig One: No. What?
>
> Enormous Crocodile: [*Grinning*] For my lunch today, I would like a nice juicy little child.

1 Read the play script of the story with a partner. Take turns to be each crocodile. Make each crocodile sound different. Remember what each crocodile is like:
- The Enormous Crocodile: mean, hungry, tricky.
- The Notsobig One: a normal crocodile, likes to eat fish, thinks the Enormous Crocodile is silly.

2 Make a sock puppet for each crocodile. You will need a pair of socks (green if possible). Add some craft eyes. Make some teeth out of white felt or paper and stick these on the sock. Make each crocodile look a bit different. Draw a background for the puppets. Perform the scene using the play script version on page 114. Remember:
- talk loudly and clearly
- try and make each crocodile sound different.

Unit 8 Highest, longest, smallest

The world's tallest buildings

Reaching for the sky

For forty years the Empire State Building was the tallest building in the world. But today, there are many buildings that are much taller.

Burj Khalifa
828 m

Shanghai Tower
632 m

Makkah Royal
Clock Tower Hotel
601 m

Empire State
Building
381 m

The Empire State Building

The Empire State Building was finished in 1931. At night it is floodlit with colourful lights. It is one of the most famous buildings in the world and has been in many films.

The Empire State building in the film *King Kong*.

Tall building facts

Name of building	Height	Year finished	City	Country
Burj Khalifa	828 m	2010	Dubai	United Arab Emirates
Shanghai Tower	632 m	2015	Shanghai	China
Makkah Royal Clock Tower Hotel	601 m	2012	Mecca	Saudi Arabia
Empire State Building	381 m	1931	New York	USA

Kingdom Tower

In 2018 there will be a new tallest building. The Kingdom Tower in Jeddah, Saudi Arabia will be an amazing 1000 m.

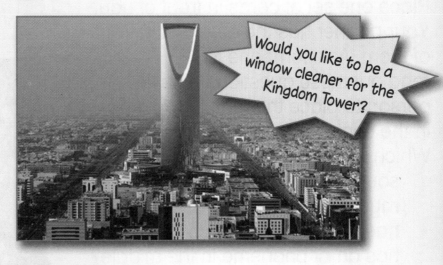

Would you like to be a window cleaner for the Kingdom Tower?

Hard stuff

Most super-tall buildings are made of steel and concrete.

Speeding up

Super-tall buildings have super-fast lifts to get to the top. The lift in Burj Khalifa can get you from the ground floor to the top in less than two minutes.

Special words

1 Practise reading these high frequency words with a partner:

> would   next   new   small
> window   there   many

Write the words on pieces of card. Create two cards for each word. Place one set of cards in front of you. Your partner has the other set in front of them. Ask someone to read out these questions. The first person to place the matching card in the centre is the winner.
Which word:

- sounds like wood?
- rhymes with bear?
- has a letter a in it which sounds e?
- has an or phoneme in the middle?

Helpful hints

Reading names
Some of the place names in the text are tricky to read. Blend the words in the brackets below to see how they are pronounced.

> Shanghai (Shang-high)
> Dubai (Doo-bigh)
> Burj Khalifa (Borsha khalifa)

2 Find these words on pages 116 and 117.

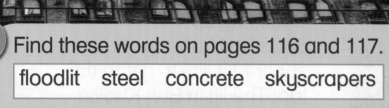

> floodlit   steel   concrete   skyscrapers

What do you think they mean?
- a See if you can work out what the word means by reading the whole sentence with a partner.
- b Ask an adult what the word means, or let them help you find the word in a dictionary.
- c Then read the sentence again to check that you understand the word.

I can spot the features of reports.

I know that different texts do different things.

Reports

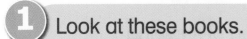

1 Look at these books.

a
How to make a kite

b

Woodland Adventure

c
All About Animals

d
What lives in the ocean?
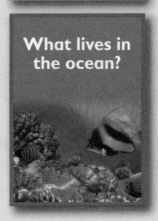

Helpful hints

Reports
Reports tell us all about something for example, all about 'Volcanoes' or 'Tallest buildings'.

- Which ones are fiction and which are non-fiction?
- Which two books do you think are reports?

2 Can you find these features in 'The world's tallest buildings' on pages 116 and 117?
- A heading – the title of the text.
- Images – pictures and photos.
- A table – with information (facts and numbers) in it.
- An introduction – the first sentences that explain what the subject is.
- A caption – a sentence that gives information about a picture.
- Present tense verbs – the action words are written in a way that tells us that these facts are happening right now.

Finding information

I can find answers by reading the text.

Helpful hints

How to read a table

Tables are a very good way of showing lots of information.

- Find the column you are interested in, for example: Height
- Find the row you are interested in, for example: Shanghai Tower
- Find the square that is in both the column and the row. This will tell you the information you need. For example, the height of the Shanghai Tower (632 m).

Name of building	Height	Year finished
Burj Khalifa	828 m	2010
Shanghai Tower	632 m	2015

1 Look through 'The world's tallest buildings' on pages 116 and 117 to find the answers to these questions:

   a   What is the name of the tallest building?

   b   When was the Empire State Building finished?

   c   How do you get to the top of these tall buildings?

   d   What will be the tallest building in 2018?

2 Use the table on page 117 to answer these questions:

   a   Which country is the Shanghai Tower in?

   b   How tall is the Empire State Building?

   c   When was the Burj Khalifa finished?

   d   Which city is the Makkah Royal Clock Tower Hotel in?

Dictionary search

1 Put these words in alphabetical order. They all start with **a** so you will need to use the second letter in the word to put them in alphabetical order.

again   air   after   am
across   and   about   along

Helpful hints

Alphabetical order
A list of words organised in the order of their first letter, for example:
apple
bat
cat

If there are two words starting with the same letter, the next letters are put in alphabetical order, for example,
a**b**le
a**c**ross
a**d**d

2 Use a dictionary to find these words that sound the same, but are spelt differently.
Read their definitions.
a root   route
b flower   flour

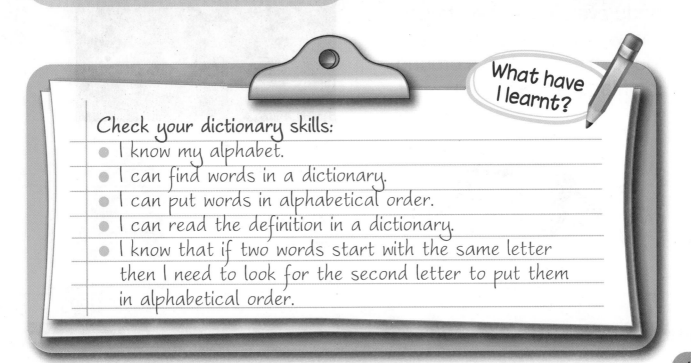

What have I learnt?

Check your dictionary skills:
- I know my alphabet.
- I can find words in a dictionary.
- I can put words in alphabetical order.
- I can read the definition in a dictionary.
- I know that if two words start with the same letter then I need to look for the second letter to put them in alphabetical order.

Micro animals

Etruscan shrew
This tiny shrew would easily fit in your hand.

The Etruscan shrew is the lightest mammal in the world.

The Etruscan shrew is a very busy little creature and is almost always moving or eating when it's not asleep. It eats insects and eats about twice the weight of its own body every day! The Etruscan shrew is quite rare but can be found in the countries around the Mediterranean Sea.

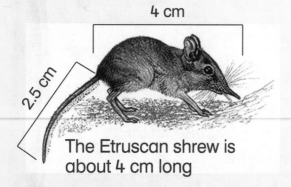

4 cm

2.5 cm

The Etruscan shrew is about 4 cm long

Glossary
predator
an animal that hunts another animal
rare
not often found
transparent
see-through
weight
the quality of being heavy

The dwarf goby
The dwarf goby is one of the smallest fish in the world. It lives in the Philippines and Singapore. It lives only for two months.

The tiny dwarf goby is almost transparent which helps it to hide from predators.

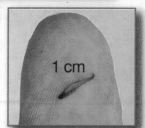

1 cm

The dwarf goby is about 1 cm long

Smallest, longest, cutest

I can spell words with the suffixes –est and –ly.

1 Read 'Micro animals' on page 122 and answer these questions.
a   How long is the Etruscan Shrew?
b   How long is a dwarf goby?
c   Why is a dwarf goby transparent?
d   How much does an Etruscan Shrew eat in a day?
e   How long does a dwarf goby live for?

2 These words all have –est at the end. Write down the root word (original word) for each one. For example, the root word of *fastest* is *fast*.
a   smallest
b   lightest
c   tallest
d   shortest

3 Add –ly or –est to these words.

> kind   quiet   lucky
> tidy   sleepy

Helpful hints

A suffix is a group of letters added to the end of a word to change its meaning.

• **est**: we add –est to an adjective to say that the object is the best or worst in that way.

> fast + est = fastest
> *John was fast but Ben was fastest.*

If the adjective ends in **y**, we change the **y** to an **i** before adding –est.

> muddy + est = muddiest
> *The Enormous Crocodile lived in the muddiest river around.*

• **–ly**: we add –ly to an adjective (describing word) when we want it to describe an action (rather than an object).

> quick + ly = quickly
> *John and Ben ran quickly to school.*

Notes about the highest mountain and longest river

Main facts

- The longest river in the world is the Nile.
- The highest mountain in the world is Mount Everest.
- Lots of people travel to Mount Everest to climb it.
- The Nile river is important to Africa for farming and for making electricity.
- Mount Everest is in Nepal and Tibet/China.
- The Nile river is in Africa and travels through ten countries.
- Mount Everest is 8848 m high.
- The Nile is 6650 km long.

Headings

- Highest mountain
- Longest river
- The Nile river
- Mount Everest

Mount Everest

Caption

- Mount Everest is also known as Sagarmatha and Chomolungma.
- The Nile river starts in Rwanda and reaches the sea in Egypt.

Extra facts

- The second tallest mountain is K2.
- The second longest river is the Amazon.

Best presentation

1 Work with a partner. Read the hints opposite and discuss them.

   a   Now create a short presentation with your partner. Choose a presentation about the Nile or Mount Everest.

   b   Choose and write down two facts on some card.

   c   Write key words on some cards, for example: Mount Everest or The Tallest mountain.

   d   Think of an introduction to your presentation.

   e   Find photographs or make drawings to illustrate your presentation.

Helpful hints

A presentation is a talk to a group of people. When we present information we:
- talk clearly
- organise the information so that it's easy to understand
- give key information
- show pictures or key words.

2

   a   Practise giving your presentation. You will need to decide:
- who will do the talking
- when you will hold up your key words and use them
- when you will say something about your pictures.

   b   Remember to talk slowly and clearly. Try to look at your audience and smile.

   c   Practise saying any difficult words often so that you do not stumble on them.

   d   Enjoy giving your presentation.

I can organise ideas.

I know the features of a report.

Planning a report

1 Read the facts on page 124 again. Use the facts to plan a report.

a Choose to write about the Nile or Mount Everest.

b Find facts to include in your report.

c Create a plan for your report. Make notes about the following:

- What **heading** will you use?
- **Pictures** – Find a photograph to print out from the internet or make your own drawings.
- What **captions** will you write for the pictures?
- An **introduction** – plan a sentence to introduce the information.
- **Main information** – which sentences will you use from page 124? You could use the extra facts to add another sentence.

Helpful hints

A **report** is a text that tells us about something. Report texts have:

- **headings**
- **pictures**
- **captions** – sentences that explain a picture
- an **introduction** – a sentence that says what the subject is
- **special words** to do with the subject.

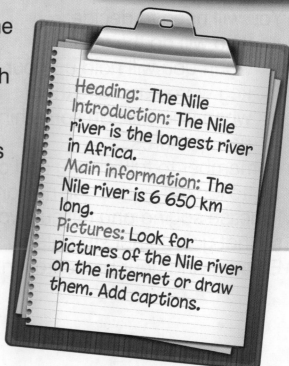

Heading: The Nile
Introduction: The Nile river is the longest river in Africa.
Main information: The Nile river is 6 650 km long.
Pictures: Look for pictures of the Nile river on the internet or draw them. Add captions.

2 Add something extra to your report.

a Find an extra fact about Mount Everest or the Nile. Find facts on the internet with an adult. Write down a new sentence on your plan.

b Make one of the sentences you have written longer by adding *and* or *because* at the end of it and finding a fact to complete the sentence. For example:

- The longest river in the world is the Nile **and** it is ...

- People travel to Mount Everest to climb it **because** ...

3

Use your plan to write your report. Use your best handwriting so that everyone can read your report.

What have I learnt?

Use this list to check your report. I have:
- used a main heading
- used capital letters and full stops
- used a picture
- used a caption
- written in the present tense
- used my best handwriting.

Book Report

Title: *When Chico Went Fishing*
Author: Robin Tzannes
Illustrator: Korky Paul

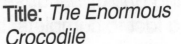

About the book:
Chico wants to go fishing, but his father doesn't think that he will sit still and won't let him join him. Miserably, Chico walks into the wood, where he makes his own fishing rod.

Why I like this book:
I like this book because of the funny illustrations.
It's good because Chico turns out to be better at fishing than his dad. My favourite bit is the picture of Chico's dad covered with fishing line.

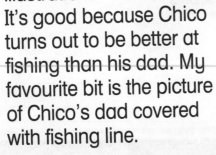

Title: *The Enormous Crocodile*
Author: Roald Dahl
Illustrator: Quentin Blake
About the book:
The Enormous Crocodile has secret plans and clever tricks so that he can catch and eat a child. Fortunately, all his plans go wrong.

Why I like this book:
This book is brilliant because the Enormous Crocodile has lots of clever tricks and just when it looks like he's going to catch a child, someone always comes and saves them. My favourite bit is when the Crocodile is thrown up into space.

24

You must read this!

1 Write a list of your four favourite books.
Talk to a partner about the books. Which book did you have the most to say about?

Helpful hints

Book reports are written by people to tell us about books they have read. They can be found in magazines and on the internet.

2 Write a book report like the one on page 128. Use the words in **bold** below to organise your report. Choose your favourite book from activity 1.

Title: The name of the book.

Author: The name of the person who wrote the book.

Illustrator: The name of the person who drew the pictures in the book. Look for it on the cover or on the first page.

About the book: Write a sentence about what the story is about. Who is the main character and what do they do in the story? You don't need to tell the whole story. For example: *Chico goes fishing even though his silly father won't let him.*

Why I like this book: Write down what you liked about the book. Was it funny, exciting, surprising? Choose one of these sentences to start:
- *I enjoyed this book because...*
- *This book is brilliant because...*
- *You must read this book because...*

Starting sentences with –ly words

I can start sentences in different ways.

1 Use these adverbs to complete the book report.

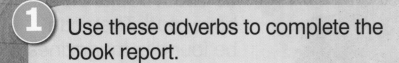

finally　　　　magically
unfortunately　　　bravely

About the book: Four children find a cupboard which _____ takes them to a different world. _____, the world is ruled by an evil witch. _____ they fight the witch and her army. Will winter _____ be over for Narnia?

Helpful hints

- Words that **end** in **–ly** tell us how something is done.

> The bird ate the worm **quickly**.

- When we put the **–ly** word at the **beginning** of a sentence, it tells us straight away that how the thing is done is really important.

> **Quickly** the bird ate the worm.

2 Write an adverb to match each meaning.

   a   all of a sudden
   b   in a happy way
   c   in a cross way
   d   at last

Suddenly,

Sharing reports

1
a Share your book report with a partner. Talk clearly and listen well.
b After listening to your partner's report, try to think of one question to ask them about the book.
c Make a note of the books that you think sound interesting.

2
a Find out which of your classmates have written about the same book. Talk about the book together and then read each other's reports. What is the same or different about them?
b Look at your report again. Can it be improved? Make any changes, then write a better version of it to be displayed.

What have I learnt?

Use this list to check your report. I have:
- written a book report
- used my best handwriting so others can read it
- used capital letters and full stops
- used interesting words to describe my book
- said why I like the book
- shared my report with others
- listened to the book reports of my classmates.

What a load of nonsense!

Omba Bolomba

Omba omba babalo pom,
Ambi pongalong, ding ding brom.
O pori, do pori slip slob slom,
Omba palomba babaloli dom.
Pin pinni lili pot?
Pin pinni plee!
Bin binni pipi lot?
Wa la pee!
Omba golomba babalo pom,
Ambika zambika zim zim zom!

By Gerard Benson

Did you know?

You're not crazy!
All the words in this poem are made up. You can read the words in the poem by segmenting and blending them – but they don't mean anything. The words are nonsense (they are meaningless) but the poem has rhythm and rhyme. We can also see that some of the sentences are questions and some are exclamations.

Nonsense – but it's a poem

1 The poem on page 132 doesn't mean anything but it still is a poem with rhyme and rhythm.
  a Find four words that rhyme with *pom*.
  b Find one word that rhymes with *plee*.
  c Some of the rhyming words are within the same line. What rhymes with:
    • Omba   • Ambika

babalo
pom

2 a Try saying these lines, clapping where the word is underlined.

> **Om**ba **om**ba **ba**balo **pom**,
> **Am**bi **pong**along, **ding** ding **brom**.

Can you clap along to the next two lines of the poem?
  b Say these lines and clap where the word is underlined.

> **Pin** pinni **li**li pot?
>   **Pin** pinni **plee**!

  c Try clapping along to these lines.

> Bin binni pipi lot?
>   Wa la pee!

3 a Find two questions in the poem.
  b Find two exclamative sentences (sentences that show strong feeling).

Reading nonsense words

1 Read the nonsense words below. Now clap each word to find out how many syllables are in it. Write and underline each syllable. The first one has been done for you.

a omba   <u>om</u> <u>ba</u>
b babalo
c pongalong
d babaloli

2 Now read the poem on page 132 aloud:

a Read each word slowly and carefully by sounding out the syllables. For example:

Am-bi-kaz-am-bi-ka

b Practise the rhythm by clapping along.
c Make the questions obvious by raising your voice at the end of the sentence. Make your voice louder at the end of exclamative sentences.
d Read the poem out loud to yourself a few times, then perform it to a friend.

Try this

Write a second line to go with one of these nonsense lines of poetry:
- dotty lotty slotty not
- ona stona crimba wim.

You could use some of the words from the first line in the second line and only change the last word. For example: dotty lotty lee.

Tongue twisters

Fat flat feet flap
Fat flat feet flip
Fat flat feet flop
Fat flat feet flit.
(Say three times quickly!)

By Michael Rosen

The Swan
Swan swam over the sea
Swim, swan, swim;
Swan swam back again
Well swam swan.
Anon

Helpful hints

A tongue twister is a poem (or a sentence) which is difficult to say. Tongue twisters are hard to say because they have lots of words starting with the same letter, or similar letters.

For example:
- Red lorry yellow lorry
- She sells sea shells on the sea shore

135

Alliteration

I can read aloud clearly.

Helpful hints

Many tongue twisters use **alliteration**. Alliteration means that two or more words start with the same phoneme or spelling pattern.

For example:
- crunchy creams
- blue blaze
- straight stripes

1 Read 'Fat flat feet flap' on page 135. This poem is a tongue twister because there are words starting **fl** and words starting just with **f** close to each other.

   a   Which word changes in each line?

   b   Write down the last word in each line. Practise saying these words loudly and clearly.

   c   Read the poem out loud, clearly and slowly. Then try saying it faster and faster (without laughing).

2 Read 'Swan swam over the sea' on page 135.

   a   How many times can you find **sw** in this poem?

   b   What is the poem about?

   c   Read the poem aloud making all the **sw** words stand out. This is difficult because the words that say **swan**, **swam** and **swum** are very similar.

3 Can you think of a word that starts with the same phoneme or spelling pattern as these words?

   a <u>l</u>ike   b <u>s</u>illy   c <u>dr</u>agon   d <u>cr</u>ow

Acrostics

Helpful hints

An **acrostic** is a poem where the first letter of each line spells a word.

Acorn

A single seed
Can feed a **squirrel**
Or grow into a giant **oak** that
Rains down new
Nuts every autumn.

by Steven Schnur

Beach

Blankets and umbrellas,
Endless miles of sand,
And the
Constant
Hum of wind and waves.

by Steven Schnur

Glossary

acorn
the seed of an oak tree

squirrel
a small red or grey furry animal which lives in trees

oak
a type of tree

Acrostic poems

1 Read the poems on page 137. Look at the first letter of each line in each poem. What word does it spell in each poem?

2 Read the poems on page 137 again.

   a In 'Acorn' can you find a word with:
- a **long** oa phoneme spelt oa
- a **long** ee phoneme spelt ee
- a **long** ai phoneme spelt ai?

   b In 'Beach' can you find a word with:
- a **long** ee phoneme spelt ea
- a **long** ai phoneme spelt a_e?

   c What two things:
- could happen to the seed in 'Acorn'
- have people brought to the beach in 'Beach'?

3 Get into a group of five.

   a Decide which poem you would like to perform.

   b Write each letter from the five letter word, ACORN or BEACH on separate pieces of card.

   c Give a letter card to each person.

   d Each person learns the line of the poem that starts with their letter.

   e Perform the poem to the class in this way:
- each person holds up their card in order of the word and says their line
- at the end of the poem the class will be able to read the word.

Writing an acrostic

a Write your own acrostic. Choose a short word about something you like. For example, *school* or *animals.* Write the word down the page like this: ➡

s a
c n
h i
o m
o a
l l
  s

b Think of a word or a phrase that starts with each letter. You can have one word per line or many words on each line, for example:

- The first line of 'School' could be:
  Shouting, skipping, sitting
- The first line of 'Animals' could be:
  All sorts of animals

You could make your poem like one long sentence:	Or it could be a list poem:
Shouting, skipping, sitting	**A**wful anaconda
Children everywhere	**N**ice newts
Hopping, jumping, laughing	**I**tchy insects
Outside at playtime	**M**ighty moose
Only five minutes until	**A**crobatic ant
Lessons begin again	**L**azy lions
	Sleepy sloth

What have I learnt?

Use this list to check your poem. I have:
- used a capital letter for the first word in each line
- written a poem that spells a word
- chosen words that start with a particular letter
- chosen words that are interesting to read
- put adjectives in my poem
- used alliteration at least once in my poem.

Shape poems

Helpful hints

Shape poems
A shape poem is a poem where the words are set out in a shape. Shape poems can have one word or lots of words.

Football

kick goal ball score in grass tackle referee Brazil Cup Germany World goal in Beckham Yay whistle goalpost time goal

Mosquito

This vampire flyer
Has one desire:
To dip its
Straw
into
yo-
ur
p
o
r
e
!

By Robert Scotellaro

Glossary

pore
the small hole in your skin that lets sweat out

Writing shape poems

1 'Mosquito' is a shape poem. The shape of the poem is part of its meaning.

a   What does the poem 'Mosquito' look like?

b   Why has the poet used this shape?

c   Who is the 'vampire flyer'?

d   Find two words that rhyme with **flyer**.

e   Find these three words that rhyme: **straw, your, pore**. What long vowel phoneme does each word have?

Helpful hints

Say the word **store**. Can you hear the **or** sound at the end of the word?

The **or** sound can be spelt:
- **or** as in **for**
- **aw** as in **paw**
- **ore** as in m**ore**
- **our** as in f**our**
- **au** as in d**au**ghter

2 Write your own shape poem.

a   Think of your favourite hobby or club, for example, football.

b   Draw a picture of an object to do with your hobby.
Look at the example of a football shirt shown on page 140.
Draw the outline of the object lightly in pencil.

c   Fill in the shape with words to do with your hobby.
For example: kick, goal, ball, score, grass, tackle, referee.
Repeat the words until the shape is filled up.

Note: You must use your neatest handwriting for your shape poem. You could pencil some lines in to help you. Make sure you keep the words a constant size and the letters correctly formed so that the words can be read.

```
o          fish, fish, fish,              swim,
    o          glass, bowl, bubbles,          seaweed,
    o    castle, silver, orange, gold, fins,  eyes, gills,
    o  scales, fast, slow, waves, ocean, tide, shells,
    slippery, fish, fish, fish, swim, glass, bowl, bubbles,
      seaweed, castle, silver, orange, gold, fins, eyes,
         gills, scales, fast, slow, waves,     fish, fish,
            tide, shells, slippery,        ocean,
                swim,                   glass
```

```
              fish, fish, fish,              swim,
    o          glass, bowl, bubbles,          seaweed,
    o    castle, silver, orange, gold, fins,  eyes, gills,
    o  scales, fast, slow, waves, ocean, tide, shells,
    o slippery, fish, fish, fish, swim, glass, bowl, bubbles,
      seaweed, castle, silver, orange, gold, fins, eyes,
         gills, scales, fast, slow, waves,     fish, fish,
            tide, shells, slippery,        ocean,
                swim,                   glass
```

QUIZ **3**

1   Write down the adjective in each of these sentences
   a   The Crocodile had secret plans.
   b   The children wanted to reach the high coconuts.
   c   The ice cream was delicious.
   d   The boy went for a long run.
   e   The story was an exciting one.

2   **Remember:**
   • The **ee** phoneme can be spelt **ee**, **ea**, **y** or **e_e**
   • The **ar** phoneme can be spelt **ar**
   • The **oa** phoneme can be spelt **oa**, **ow** or **o_e**
   • The **ur** phoneme can be spelt **ur**, **er** or **ir**
   • The **igh** phoneme can be spelt **igh**, **y** or **i_e**
   • The **ow** phoneme can be spelt **ow** or **ou**
   • The **ai** phoneme can be spelt **ai**, **ay** or **a_e**
   Draw a table like this. Add the words in the bubble below
   to the correct column in the table.

ee	ar	oa	ur	igh	ow as in cow and out	ai
green	dark					

feet green inside out around away dark garden grow even
girl each hard boat cried down car please our baby birds

3   Add −est or −ly to the end of these words.
   fair   slow   weak
   poor   strong   warm